D1745421

# Birding the Santa Monica Mountains

# Birding the Santa Monica Mountains

## Gerry Haigh

Illustrated by Jillian Palethorpe

Cover photographs by Ken Wheeland

Hillside Press    Fairbanks, Alaska

Copyright © 2008 by Gerry Haigh

All rights reserved. No part of this book may be reproduced or trans-
mitted in any form or by any means, electronic or mechanical, including
photocopying, recording, or by any information storage and retrieval
system, without permission in writing from the author.

This edition was prepared for printing by
Ghost River Images
5350 East Fourth Street
Tucson, Arizona 85711
www.ghostriverimages.com

Illustrations by Jillian Palethorpe

ISBN 978-0-9627530-3-9

Library of Congress Control Number: Pending

Printed in the United States of America

First Printing: May, 2008

10 9 8 7 6 5 4 3 2 1

# Contents

Part 3
More Thoughts on the Cowbird

Part 4
Raptors

# Foreword

The material in this book first appeared in the *Messenger*, The Santa Monica Mountains News and Arts Publication, Topanga, California.

"Get in on the Wild!" was the first article in the Topanga Wild series. These columns contained essays and poems about personal experiences with birds and wildlife in the Santa Monica Mountains.

# Topanga Wild
### Get in on the Wild!

Topanga! Where the mountains meet the sea. Or, more profoundly, where Western culture meets the natural world.

Why do we live here?

Outsiders don't understand why we are willing to risk the recurrent threat of fires and floods. How can they know that fires and floods are an essential part of why we are here? We put them together with the annual explosion of wild flowers in the spring, the nightly keening of coyotes, the incessant din of mating frogs, the booming of the owl, the screeching of the hawk... all these and many more are among the natural forces which draw us to these Santa Monica Mountains. For most of us, is it not a primary pupose in living here to reconnect with our roots in the earth?

And our children lead the way.

On his way home from school Alan came up out of the creek, eyes wide with excitement, exclaimed "I saw a deer, Dad."

Teachers affirm that our children are unique in the way they are tuned in to nature. Five-year-olds pick up snakes. A seven-year-old keeps a list of the birds she has seen in Topanga.

We share our property with the birds and animals. We carry on decades-long fights against development companies and big corporations to preserve as much land as possible in its pristine state.

Topangans tend to have strong commitments to the wild–both for appreciating and protecting it.

# Introduction

*How I Became a Birder*

"You can lead a horse to water, but…"

My mother took me to the water and I have been drinking ever since. When I was about seven, she took me to the shore of the Hudson River to show me a hill profusely covered with Wild Columbine. Awestruck at this dazzling, scarlet display, I was drinking in the beauty of the flowers when a raucous commotion erupted behind me. I turned to see a large flock of blackbirds settling in the reeds near shore. As they jostled for position, they were flashing bright red epaulets, the same scarlet color as the Columbines.

The intense red on the hill–the bright red in the marsh all seemed magical to me. It remains one of the most vivid memories of my childhood and has helped fuel my lifelong interest in birds.

This sighting was very impactful, but my "First Bird" in the sense of the one which launched me into serious birding was a Starling! It seems strange, now, that this "trash bird" was ever the object of an exciting new discovery for me. The Starling and the English Sparrow were the two most common birds in New York City and were often called "trash birds."

My discovery began when Mrs. Burgess, my fifth grade teacher, assigned our class the project of compiling a nature study book. The part I remember best is the section on birds. She gave us a list and asked us to get a picture of each bird to put in our journal. All but one of the pictures I needed I found on cards put out by the Arm and Hammer baking soda company. The only bird not included on those cards was the Starling. I had never seen a Starling or a picture of one so I was stymied.

One day while we were visiting my grandmother in Highland Falls, my mother recognized a Starling high in the plum tree alongside the house. Mother and I rushed upstairs and found that we could see the coveted bird through a bedroom window. It was only ten feet away and at eye level. I can see it still, perched in profile; black with a purple sheen; white dots on the body; yellow bill. It looked exotic and very handsome. After it flew, I set to work with drawing paper and colored pencils and drew a picture of it.

The image of that Starling is still very clear to me as I write about it a lifetime later. I remember that that drawing was for me the centerpiece of my whole nature study book.

Afterwards, at my urging, my mother retrieved from the attic an ancient pair of opera glasses and a field guide by Chester A. Reed both of which she had used in college and which she then gave to me. I was launched into my lifetime hobby as a birder and along the way became the Birdman of Topanga!

**Part 1**

# Topanga Winter
# July-November

# Where the Mountains Meet the Sea
### Written after a drought which lasted for five years

"Topanga", they say, is where
the mountains meet the sea.
Where the mountains meet the sea
is where the earth gives birth to life.
Where the mountains meet the sea
is where the children play;
Perhaps in unconscious celebration
of that miraculous conception.

For five long years
Topanga has been thirsting
for the life-sustaining fluid.
Far too long her hills have been covered
with vast stretches of dead weeds.

Finally the sea has been bountiful.
It has sent us saturated emissaries
to pour their precious cargo over the thirsty earth.
In eleven drenching days
our mountains exuberantly received
twenty-two inches of rain.

The woodland luxuriated
in steady, soaking showers.
Washed clean of accumulated dust,
every leaf on every tree and shrub glistened in radiant appreciation.
Every stem was studded
with strings of diamond drops.

The streambeds were voluptuously full
of milky chocolate fluid
dashing madly back to sea.
The sound space was filled
with the roar of rushing water,
boiling around boulders,
cascading over fallen trees,
gushing through fissures.

Everywhere the soil sucked in the vital fluid.
Nourished deep within itself,
it sent back to the surface
a billion blades of grass.
A million subtle shoots
thrust rudely through the ground
to rise up and punctuate
the spreading sea of grass.
All of the shoots will ultimately flower.

Already the Peony is lush with buds.
The Wild Cucumber grows a foot a day.
Milk Maids dance in the glades along the banks of streams.
Buckthorn blossoms cover the hills
like a mantle of snow.
A myriad of other flowers is
about to burst into bloom.

We, the people of Topanga,
carriers of consciousness for the planet,
(perhaps for the universe)
marvel at the wonder of the rebirth all around us
where the mountains meet the sea.

# Kitchen Garden Morning

I look into our garden this morning.
At the far end of our yard
is a feeding station around which the birds gather.
Background music is provided
by a family of coyotes in the hills beyond
who lift their quavering voices in eerie serenade.
A pair of Spotted Towhees
are front and center below the feeder,
showing off their rich auburn sides,
black heads,  and backs with bright white designs.
A pair of Scrub Jays fly in,
the Towhees retreat into the nearby shrubs,
a gray Titmouse with jaunty crest
is pecking at the seeds in the feeder.
Until a very handsome male Acorn Woodpecker
takes over the field,
flashing a bright red crown
and startling black and white plumage.
Song Sparrow. Brown Towhees. Bewick's Wren.
House Finches. Mourning Doves.
Another day has begun.

# This Mostly Brown Meadow

This mostly brown meadow which displayed
so many bright flowers
to dazzle us in the spring
has to be studied carefully now
to spot a thin sprinkling of Purple Clarkia here,
a wrinkled patch of Tarweed there,
a withered stand of Gumweed elsewhere.
The birds also seem to find this place drab
and sound depressed about it.
A Nuttall's Woodpecker starts his rattle
but doesn't complete it.
A Towhee emits his first note and stops.
A Titmouse pecks lethargically on a branch but withholds his
song for a more promising setting.
A Raven moans mournfully in the distance,
but only for a short time.

Must I remain wrapped in this gray gloom?
Dare I betray my heavy heart
by gazing on the lovely green hills
or flicking my attention to the dancing
of the weeds in the breeze?

16

I seem more true to myself
by feeling sorry for myself
for being abandoned
by these miserable birds and flowers
in this miserable meadow.
My stance is confirmed as I stand to leave
and find a tick embedding itself
in a tender part of my anatomy.

# Winter

Someone reminded me that this is the last day of summer. It doesn't feel like the last day of summer. It feels like we are in the midst of winter. The meadows which stretch before me are brown and lead. No colorful blooms are visible. Of course, this isn't 'real' winter. Rather it's Topanga winter.

The seasons initially get defined for us by the place which we regard as our childhood homeland. For me, that place is New York State where the image of winter features bare hardwood trees, frozen ground and sometimes snow. Its time frame coincides with when winter is supposed to be according to the conventional calendar.

After years in California I find I no longer know what winter is at all. I drift in my mind between east and west, between New

York and Topanga. Eastern winter, I remind myself, runs between December 22 and March 21. But Topanga winter begins in August when the meadows turn brown and very dry and lasts until the rains come in late December or January.

Our winter here is not only different in its timing, but also in its impact on peoples' consciousness. Easterners worry about blizzards. Topangans are fearful of fires. While New Englanders grimly endure nor'easters, we nervously endure the Santanas. They measure their discomfort in degrees of coldness while we measure ours in degrees of heat, particularly as it approaches the combustion point. (Our cultural definition of Hell must have come from a people with a climate similar to ours.)

The bird population includes migrants such as the Wilson's Warbler, Yellow Warbler, Townsend's Warbler, Yellow-breasted Chat and Rufous Hummingbird; winter residents such as the Yellow-rumped Warbler (Butterbut, for short), Ruby-crowned Kinlet, Golden-crowned Sparrow, plus our abundant supply of year-round residents like the two species of Towhee, the Wrentit, the Thrasher, the Lark Sparrow, etc.

We have a greater variety and a greater number of 'winter' birds. One factor contributing to this is that eastern winter comes later and all the migrating birds have come through. Our winter comes precisely at the time all the migrants are coming through.

# Walk among the Oaks

I walk among the wild oaks
which so snugly cover our mountains.
They wantonly spread their limbs
every which way but up and proper
like trees are supposed to do.
Their careless ways
create seductive tangles
which lure wild creatures
to pockets created inch by inch
over a period of years.
The minuscule pace of this evolution
is hardly understood
by the animals which enjoy its results
but whose own movements
are measured in seconds.

Soft sounds welcome me to the wild.
The chip-chip-chip trill of the Wrentit
is the first that I hear,
a repetitive background song.

The chatter of a nearby Titmouse
sounds like she's trying
to make friendly contact with me.
The far off calls of a few crows
is their way of staying in touch with each other.
The weeds are whistling in a breeze
or is that my Tinitis[1]?

---

[1] A medical condition causing a constant ringing in the ears.

# Dead Meadow: Starving Insects

Though there is a hardly a drop of nectar
in an acre of dead weeds,
The starving butterfly
continues to propel himself
into passing gusts of wind.
But the weed he is dropped onto
is as dead as the one he left.
A dragonfly propels himself about,
but his flights are equally fruitless.

# The Wind and the Gong

The gong which hangs beside our back door
gives a voice to the wind.
It is also true that the wind
gives a voice to the gong.
Is it possible that they have
any awareness of what they do for each other?
Or do we humans have to carry awareness
for these two
and a million other miscellanea in the universe?

# A Walk in the Weedy Woodland

As we near the end of August
I note in my journal
that we have had no rain
since the beginning of May.
And yet, as I walk this woodland trail,
I am protected from the hot sun
by a sweet canopy of green.
I quietly thank the trees
for sending their roots down deep enough
to tap a water supply
which keeps their leaves green.

When I look down at the ground,
I see that all the grasses
have turned to weeds
and the overall view
is brown and dead.
Suddenly a miracle appears
at my feet.
A tiny flash of scarlet
just a half inch above the ground
turns out to be a flower
the size of my thumbnail.
I recognize it as an Indian Pink.
(Its name is not for its color
but for its shape.

The petals are pinked
as if nature had cut them
with pinking shears.)
Another half mile down the trail
I am drawn to another flash of color.
This one is bright orange,
a little larger than the Pink
and at the end of a long stem
which it bends so that
it almost touches the dirt.
I recognize it as Gumweed
and press a finger into the bloom
to check the stickiness
which confirms its identity.
These two small ones, the only flowers I saw
blooming on my morning walk,
MADE MY DAY!

# Beware of Careless Beauty

On a much too hot day
I slump in my box canyon.
A very lazy breeze
gently stirs the leaves
for a very short while.
When the scene settles back into
hot and still,
I make a little discovery.
Near the foot of the cliff,
where winter water will fall again
I spot a bright red leaf
nestling in some spider webs.
I'm reaching out to pluck this jewel
when I suddenly pull back, muttering:
"Why does the only splash of
attractive color
in this whole dismal scene
have to be Poison Oak?"

# Birds On the Move.

Sunlight poured into the canyon
behind our house,
highlighting a very attractive landscape
of bushes and trees swaying slightly
in a gentle breeze.
No sooner did the scene light up
with the arrival of the sun
when a flock of warblers and flycatchers
also poured into the canyon.
These birds were never still.
At any given moment
a half dozen were aloft, twisting, turning
and deftly snatching insects from the air.
Then they would magically disappear in the foliage
as they were replaced by another platoon.

continues

The feeding frenzy was very understandable:
These were migrating birds and had flown
perhaps four hundred miles the night before
and would fly as far the next night,
so they must replenish
their energy resources.
Later when the fickle sun
disappeared behind a cloud,
the birds also disappeared,
seemingly into the shadows on the hillside.
When the sun furtively
crept back down the hillside,
the birds failed to return,
seeking, perhaps, a more reliably
lit-up canyon
and a steady supply of insects in the air.

# No Raptors in Raptor Meadow
(report of sightings in the middle of an August day in Topanga)

Since this is August, it is now winter in this Topanga meadow. Brown, brown, brown everywhere... the entire meadow is filled with dead weeds. The only bright color is provided by a scattering of Gumweed blossoms on otherwise withered plants.

In contrast with the prevailing presence of death in the meadow, the bordering oak trees are green and healthy. Perhaps you might expect me to run away from the prevailing presence of death in the meadow and off into the arboreal greenery but I find the meadow's deadness profoundly peaceful. The sky today is uniformly gray and I can imagine sitting against a rock and gazing all around me, my eyes lazily taking in broad swaths of brown and gray and gradually drifting into a soul-solacing tranquility.

The path I walked is filled with scat deposited by dogs and coyotes in a mass ratio of ten to one. Obviously, there isn't much food here to attract the wild canines, whereas their domestic cousins come here only for their daily exercise and are fed amply indoors.

Birds are in scarce supply this 'winter' day. The complete

absence of raptors is particularly notable. It has not been unusual for birders to find as many as four or five species within an hour here. Two pairs of White-tailed Kites nested here this past breeding season along with Cooper's Hawks, Red-shouldered Hawks, Red-tailed Hawks. Harriers hang around the meadow until it is time for them to go north to nest. These rodent-filled acres have been aptly named for the raptors which have adopted them.

So strange not to see a single raptor in Raptor Meadow! Birds in general are very scarce. I hear one Wrentit sing, see one Brown Towhee and nothing else until I reach a far corner of the meadow and encounter two flocks, one of Bushtits, the other Lesser Gold-finches. The Bushtits are feeding in oak trees on the border. The Goldfinches are feeding on dead weeds, nearby. Bushtits have tiny bills, suitable for snatching up insects when the little guys are preening leaves. The Finches have sturdy bills which can crack seeds for sustenance. The meadow is not dead for these two!

# Meadow After a Firestorm

Over the wide sweep of meadow
all is ashen memorial
to the fury of the firestorm.

The flames that flared so briefly;
terrifying, beautiful,
exhilarating, deadly;
have left their runic mark
upon the land.

Testimony to their magic
is given in the long silence
where autumn browns, reds and yellow
were transformed into shades of gray;
and bushes, branches, grass, and trees
were transformed into grains of grit.

Now no lizards scamper about,
no ants scurry, no spiders stride.
Only the bleached skull of a ground squirrel
and a few empty white snail shells
adorn this scarred and sacred ground.
Here is both a cemetery
and a seedbed for preparing
next spring's bright assault.

# Sightings in a Dry Season

I celebrated the summer solstice with a two-mile hike on the Backbone Trail off Old Topanga Canyon. The wilderness I encountered was severely impacted by the frightening drought we have been experiencing. Checking my records, I find that our last rains were in March with a total of .3 inches. In February we had 1.3 inches and in January a total of 1.6 inches, with a grand total of 3.2 inches for all of 2002. While all of our trees are still green, courtesy of roots going deep underground, the surface of the meadows presented me with a canvas of unrelenting brown dead weeds, with a handful of widely scattered flowers. One was a single blossom of Morning Glory which magically burst into my awareness along the path and, for the first time in my experience, it clearly justified its somewhat pretentious name.

I also thrilled to four or five clusters of Gumweed, the most abundant flower of the day. Its golden face seemed very friendly, seeming to invite me to feel its stickiness, which I fingered a number of times.

Finally I came upon one small patch of Cliff Aster which presented me with its dashing bouquet of numerous pink and white petals. It was strikingly apparent to me how scarcity enormously enhances the appeal of objects. Think of the high value we place on rare gems; each of my few flowers seen seemed like a jewel in its own right.

Birds were almost as scarce as flowers in this barren landscape. Topanga's most omnipresent bird, the crow, was conspicuously absent. I heard the sibilant whining of two Red-tailed Hawk youngsters, full size undoubtedly, but not able to hunt yet, calling upon their parents to feed them. I heard a Red-shouldered Hawk calling its mate. I heard a few birds which remained hidden and unable to be identified by me. I saw a pair of Towhees running along the path and finally into the bushes.

Then, near the end of my hike, I came upon the highlight of the day! Flitting about in the bare lower branches, so close I didn't even raise my binoculars to look at it, was a Blue-gray Gnatcatcher. Almost as small as a wren, he was exceedingly handsome with his black crown, white eye ring, bright blue back, gray and white flanks and underparts. His call has been described as squeaky like a mouse and not much louder, but his song is exquisite and is described by John Burroughs as so faint, it is as if the bird is singing in its sleep.

I know the Gnatcatcher to be a very pugnacious fighter. I have seen him drive off a Cooper's Hawk, at least ten times his size, from his nesting area. His color pattern is very similar to the gray and white of the mockingbird, which also aggressively deals with offending hawks and crows. Is there something about that color pattern which endows the wearer with special courage? Another parallel for the Gnatcatcher is his size similarity to our smallest but also toughest winged creature, the hummingbird. Our anthropomorphic reaction to that is to suggest a "little guy complex" within the avian world.

My Gnatcatcher seemed very friendly to me, almost as if he appreciated my company in this desolate woodland. I certainly appreciated his and preferred to linger as long with him as he was willing to with me. However, his mate called from the bushes on the other side of the path and he flew across to join her.

When I climbed into my car about ten minutes later, I found myself still joyful over my brief encounter with my bird of the day.

*Cooper's Hawk*

# Dry Solitude

I am walking on a trail
in the woodland hills of home.
I come to a clearing.
Two deer are browsing
on an impoverished patch of lawn.
They look exceedingly thin.
Their need to stay
with the small piece of green
allows me to get quite close.
When they begin to retreat
I back off a few paces
to give them their space.

Movement in the trees
on the far edge of the clearing
attracts my attention:
I gradually make out
a large mixed flock
of silent little birds.
Silence in fact prevails
in this entire wilderness scene
as if I had happened upon
a woodland worship service
devoted to silent prayer,
the celebrants flit,
tip-toe-ingly about.

continues

A woodpecker's soft chatter,
a Wrentit's delicate trill
are beautiful solo performances
against the background of serene silence.
But when a Scrub Jay
blasts out a raucous screech,
it strikes me as terribly inappropriate.

Profound silence is immediately reestablished
While the Jay flies nervously away.
Is he embarrassed about his goof?
Or is he simply bored?

Walking on around the deer
I happen upon a lone Towhee
ravishing dry seed pods,
many of which abound
in this drought-driven land.
The solitary, melancholy bird,
a somber shade of brown
in a landscape of dead leaves,
unexpectedly bursts into song.
Energy in the seeds is transformed
into food for the soul!

Farther along the trail
I encounter a pair of Towhees
industriously pecking away
at scant forage on the ground.
One of them goes off the trail
into some heavy underbrush.
Just before disappearing into the shadows
it flips up its tail,
flashing a maroon patch
the one bit of color on a Towhee,
its way of signaling to its mate
"Here I go–follow me."

I am feeling very weary.
I seek out a tree,
Slump down on the ground against it.
I look up at the sky,
clear and blue
and very far away.
I sit without waking,
look without seeing,
I drift into reverie. I become pure energy
setting forth with speed of light
through an infinity of space
and an eternity of time
taking me to an edge of the universe.

continues

If I look back toward home,
Will I find that my fellow earthlings
have finally given up hating each other-
and killing each other?

Will they finally learn to love each other
And to live in peace?
If I decide to undertake this journey,
Will You promise me a happy ending,
Dear God?

# Golden Leaves

Golden leaves
clinging to trees
Rustling in the breeze.

Golden leaves
Drifting down
carpeting the ground.

Golden leaves
come to rest
on the earth's firm breast,

Opening wide our arms,
we gather up this golden treasure
to gild the barren days with pleasure.

# Dead Sea

A brown mantle of meadow
spreads somberly over a hill.
A sparse sprinkling of yellow blooms
are lonely signs of life
in a dead sea of weeds.
A single swallow speeds swiftly overhead
Following a straight line,
and is quickly gone.
Crows call in the distance
but none venture into view.
I bear witness to the kingdom of the dead
and am content.

# The Birds of Winter

For thousands of years, birds have been coming south in winter to the Santa Monica Mountains. The mountains themselves rose up out of the sea, like Venus, at least a million years ago. When the mountains established themselves as land masses, birds were already abundant on Planet Earth, having evolved 140 million years before.

The rise of our mountains coincided roughly with the beginning of the Pleistocene Ice Age. Glaciers covered the western part of the North American continent down into the state of Washington and throughout the Sierras. The animal population of all the northern states and all of Canada must have been driven into Oregon, California, Mexico and Central America. When the glaciers retreated 10,000 years ago, many of the birds returned north. These movements of birds in relation to ice, going south with advancing glaciers and north with retreating glaciers, is thought to have contributed to the development of migration patterns which continue to this day.

The last glacial retreat occurred 10,000 years ago. Up to that time a million and a half bird species had evolved on Planet Earth. Fewer than 9,000 species exist today. Life is everchanging. As conditions change, old species die out and new ones emerge. How long will our own species survive? We have only been around for four or five million years. Will we last as long as the great horned owl, which has already survived for 60 million years?

The birds which travel down here to the Santa Monicas for the winter in our time have probably been doing so for 10,000 years. That is also thought to be when the first North Americans crossed the Bering Strait and began moving down the continent, reaching this region at least 7,000 years ago. Since we know that the earliest Californians depended on all forms of wildlife, we can safely say that people have been observing the seasonal fluctuations in Topanga birds for some 7,000 years.

December has come back to Topanga along with the White-crowned Sparrows, the Butterbutts and the rain. Of the four, only December is precisely predictable, depending as it does on the very regular movements of our highly dependable planet which has revolved around our star at a steady rate approximately four and a half billion times.

Not much in the natural world arrives on the same day every year, certainly not birds or rain. Weather, of course, is notoriously unreliable. During the last twelve years, the first rain of the season fell over a range of ninety-five days spread out from August through November.

Bird movements are about as unpredictable as the weather. Take the White-crowned Sparrow, a representative avian winter resident in our town. During the last ten years, there were not two years during which they arrived on the same day. First sightings ranged over 93 days and spread from October through January, about the same variance as we found in the rainfall.

*Yellow-rumped Warbler*

So it's December and the Butterbutts are back. So what? What are Butterbutts? You won't find the name in any of the bird books; but any birder will tell you that "Butterbutts" is the affectionate nickname for the Yellow-rumped Warbler. Try saying the two names aloud and notice how much easier one slips out. That makes a significant difference when you realize how often the name is used by birders in our area during the winter season of October through April! During much of that time it is the most frequently seen bird. Often there are over a million Butterbutts in the Santa Monicas.

Returning to the first profound question in the preceding paragraph ("So what?"), the arrival of the Butterbutts and the White-crowns reflects the coming and going of birds in general. These two are among the twenty-five species which frequently winter with us in Topanga. Both of the species breed as far north as the northernmost limits of the boreal forests in Alaska and Canada. However, both also breed in the Sierra Mountains. So we don't know if the Butterbutt we see at Trippet Ranch has come from as far as 3,000 miles in linear distance or 10,000 feet of altitudinal distance.

We Angelenos are accustomed to having visitors throng our resorts throughout the winter. A major factor contributing to this influx is our adjoining ocean which insures a mild climate and beaches on which to enjoy sunny days.

While tourists pour in by the thousands, birds are pouring in by the millions. Climate only indirectly influences this influx of avian visitors. The mild weather in itself is no big deal for birds, but it does ensure a good food supply via a profusion of insects and meadows loaded with seeds which are not covered with ice and snow. Another major factor is the incorporation of a mountain range within the city limits. The Santa Monicas provide a vast expanse of woodlands and chaparral where the birds can hang out without much disturbance from us hominids.

So when you have had enough of gawking at the tourists who flood our beaches and boulevards, traipse through the hills with a pair of binoculars and see how many of our winged visitors you can identify.

*Topanga Wildflowers*

# Winter Visitors: The Snow Birds of Topanga

Our mild Mediterranean climate in Southern California has accustomed us to having winter visitors from harsher climes. Our winter freeways abound in cars displaying license plates from Illinois, New York, Alaska and the like. Similarly, our winter wilderness areas abound with birds sporting plumage denoting Oregon, Canada, Alaska to the experienced birder.

Just as winter weather in northern regions induces many people to head for California and Florida, so it also induces many birds to migrate long distances, some from as far north as the arctic tundra all the way to the plains of Patagonia in South America. However, while people are responding to the coldness itself, birds are not so bothered by the cold, but go south because of the reduced food supply.

Some avian long-distance migrants may spend a few days resting and feeding in Topanga and then move on to Central and South America. Many migrants fly high overhead at night and we never see them in Topanga.

Finally, there is another group which finds conditions ideal for spending the winter right here in the Santa Mountains, and these are the ones we are apt to see from October through April.

### Yellow-rumped Warbler

The most abundant of our winter residents is the Yellow-rumped Warbler. Some winters there may be as many as a million in the Santa Monicas. They are usually found in small flocks, feeding on seeds or insects, in bushes or in the canopy of trees. We watched one skating on the pond at Trippet Ranch one winter. It would run and slide to a stop, then pick up a seed. It kept doing this over and over again as if it were learning to skate. When this warbler flies away from you, look for the flashing yellow runp.

### Dark-eyed Junco

The Dark-eyed Junco is our next most abundant winter visitor. Occasionally a few pairs stay with us year round to raise their young. One year, a pair nested in a flowerpot at Camp Wildwood. All winter we may see small flocks of Juncos feeding on the ground anywhere in Topanga. When they fly away, one can usually see their white outer tail feathers flashing.

### White-crowned Sparrow

The White-crowned Sparrow is another gregarious ground feeder. Like the Junco, it sometimes visits our feeders. The black and white stripes on the crown give the adult bird a striking appearance.

*Hermit Thrush*

## *Hermit Thrush*

The Hermit Thrush has earned its name through solitary habits. It differs from the three preceding birds in not gathering in flocks of its own kind. On its breeding grounds, it has perhaps the most beautiful song in North America, but while with us, it never utters more than a one-note call. It feeds on the ground and may be identified by its rufous tail and the large brown spots on its breast.

## *Ruby-crowned Kinglet*

The Ruby-crowned Kinglet is another loner. It is the size of a Bushtit, which by contrast is almost always found in flocks. The Kinglet has a characteristic habit of repeatedly flicking its shoulders. Despite the bird's name, do not expect to see a ruby crown, because the male seldom displays that showy monument.

Although the Kinglet and the Hermit Thrush avoid their own kind, they frequently travel in mixed-species flocks which may include Sparrows, Juncos, Titmice and Towhees. These flocks move through the chaparral and oak groves, with each species feeding in its own unique way, and all helping each other finding food and guarding against predators.

All of these wintering birds breed as far north as the northernmost parts of Alaska and Canada. However, all of them also nest in the Sierra. When we see them here, we don't really know if their journey had best be measured in thousands of miles of linear distance or in thousands of feet of altitude change.

Most of our winter visitors will be with us until March or April, when they will go back up-mountain or up-continent. They spend about six month here and six months there.

Are we justified in claiming them as "our" birds which go away to nest, or are they "their" birds which come here to winter?

# Encounter Across a Swath of Dead Meadow

There are around here
only two representatives
of life forms on a higher plane
than lizards and insects.

They are eying each other
across a swath of dead meadow,
each perched in a manner
comfortable for its body structure.

One is gripping a dead branch
at the top of an Elderberry bush
in an otherwise treeless plain.
He can see and be seen in every direction.

The other is sitting on the ground.
He can see and be seen
in only one direction,
on a sight line with the bush.

continues

One looks at the other with admiration.
The other looks back warily.
One names the other, noting the name in a notebook.
The other neither knows names nor possesses a notebook.

The man records his sighting
of the Black Prince of the Chaparral.
The Phainopepla keeps apprehensive vigil
over a potentially dangerous human.

# Rare Visitors from the Mountaintops

Three inches of rain fell last night. The fall was so gentle and the earth so thirsty that not a drop overflowed. There was dampness everywhere but no riding on the chair lifts at Mammoth and June Lake.

We remembered one time when we had watched a Nutcracker digging deep into the snow and were surprised to see him come up with a pine cone seed.

We learned later that the Clark's Nutcracker sometimes forages in snow as deep as eight inches, puddles and all. The clouds and the earth were tender lovers, each filling the other's need—the one to give, the other to receive. This morning both the land and the sky are clear, clean, and refreshed.

A Wrentit trills to her mate nearby. He chip-chip-brrs back. Lifelong partners, they patrol the brush together, never leaving their two-acre homestead. My wife and I have extended our own homestead to include this mesa along which we are sauntering. Like the earth and the sky and the Wrentit pair, we are another bonded couple in this natural panorama.

Well into our stroll, our attention is suddenly riveted by the appearance of a flock of birds which may have never before been seen in this particular place. Fifteen Clark's Nutcrackers fly silently across the fire road not more than twenty feet from us. This is a bird we know from high in the Sierra. Lynne has a passion for the peaks, so we have been there often and Nutcrackers have always been part of our mountain experience. We knew them as the only bird we were apt to see foraging above tree-line, but never had we ever seen or expected to see them in Topanga!

We saw this flock for only as long as it took them to cross the road and disappear over a ridge beside it. We ran up the ridge but they had disappeared and we never saw them again.

The Nutcracker is named after Captain William Clark, having been discovered for the Western world during the Lewis and Clark expedition. When Thomas Jefferson sent Lewis and Clark west, he directed them not only to discover and map out the geography of the vast lands comprising the Louisiana Purchase, but also to study the peoples and the natural history which they discovered for Western culture. Another bird, a woodpecker, was named after Lewis. It is interesting to note that the only two birds named after the leaders of the expedition were involved in a mix-up in identification. The Nutcracker, which is a member of the Crow family was thought to be a Woodpecker, and the Woodpecker was thought to be a Crow! This confusion is not so surprising when you know that the Lewis' Woodpecker (a few usually winter in the Santa Monica Mountains) is an all black bird about the size of a Crow and the Nutcracker has a large bill which he sometimes uses like a Woodpecker.

Our sighting of these birds on the mesa stirred up memories of times we had watched them in the mountains. A favorite type of viewing was while they regularly gathered pinion nuts in the late summer and buried them in the dirt, for retrieval in the winter or early spring when the site is covered with snow. In one study, it was discovered that a bird may bury as many as 33,000 pinion seeds in caches of four or five seeds each. That adds up to six to eight thousand sites. The fact that they remember most of these locations over a period of several months represents a feat of memory outstanding in the whole animal kingdom. Studies have shown that they apparently make an inner map in their mind in which they use sticks, stones and other objects to fix where to probe.

Our Scrub Jay uses a similar method of hiding and retrieving food but it is much less' efficient than the Nutcracker. For example, the Jay can carry only one seed at a time in its bill; The Nutcracker has a pouch built into its body under the tongue in which it can store up to forty seeds. Furthermore, despite the fact that it does not have to contend with snow, the Jay seems to have comparatively little memory for relocating seeds and therefore ends up providing a seeding service more advantageous for our Live Oaks than for the birds. Most of the seeds remain buried in the ground and some eventually surface as young trees. But not to worry — there is far more food readily available during winter in the Santa Monicas than in the High Sierra, so the Scrub Jay easily survives despite his careless storage practices.

I expect that whenever Lynne and I approach this part of the trail in the future, we will always remember the Clark's Nutcrackers we saw here. The connection will enrich the meaning of the trail for us. This phenomenon probably explains why I seldom seek out new paths to travel, but prefer to return to ones with lots of associations. For example, on this trail I once saw the only Mountain Quail I have seen below a four-thousand-foot altitude. Here I also saw my first Sage Sparrow running in front of me along the border of the bushes. I had to look it up in a field guide to name it. Here the

Prickly Phlox used to put out a brilliant pink display early every spring. (There are only a few of these plants left.)

As we make connections, we become bonded with a place. Our visiting birds from the mountaintops made a vivid impression on us and strengthened our bond with this part of our extended homestead. The stronger our bond with the earth, the more we feel at home in the universe.

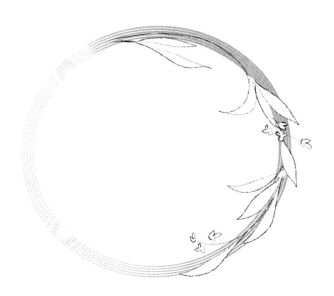

Part Two:

# The Breeding Season:
# When the Rains Begin

# Flowers

Blue Larkspurs are unfolding
their lovely intricate blossoms
sprinkling our meadows
with the latest luster of this lush year.
Last week's entrant in the floral beauty pageant
was the Nettle Lupine;
tall, proud, erect and solitary.

Each plant takes its turn in flaunting its great beauty.
Milk Maids and Wild Peony;
Purple Nightshade, Prickly Phlox;
Chocolate and Mariposa Lilies-
Each has its moment of bursting forth
from modest green
to a luminous display of gorgeous color.

The Earth has gone all out this spring
in showering all these generous gifts
on this place which we call home.

# The Swallows Return to Topanga

Much has been made of the return of the swallows to the Mission at San Juan Capistrano. Legend has it that they return on the same day every year, namely on March 19. Apparently they take leap year into account in maintaining their regularity since I have never heard that the expected date of their arrival is one day different every fourth year.

Some doubt about the validity of this legend was once raised by Jack Smith, the esteemed columnist for the Los Angeles Times. The year he went down to the mission on March 19, he found multitudes of tourists and pigeons overflowing the premises but nary a swallow in sight. He called the town's Chamber of Commerce the next day to ask if perchance the swallows had made their appearance in the evening after he had left. He was assured that of course the swallows had arrived because they always arrived on the appointed day.

Leaving aside the question of validity, there is no question about the kind of aura that a myth of this nature lends to the reputation of a community. A place singled out by wild creatures for an annual homecoming consistently coordinated with man's calendar gains a special spiritual quality.

Would that our own fair city of Los Angeles might take on some such aura. Instead, we have been smeared with a reputation for phoniness reflected in such appellations as "La-la-land" and the like. Our association with the movies leads easily to the assumption that we are more involved with contrived images than with simple, wholesome, down to earth reality.

By way of broadening our image to include more of a spiritual quality, I propose that one thing we can do is latch onto the swallow legend which has done so much to establish the Capistrano Mission as a divinely blessed place. I am not suggesting that we steal their legend but merely that we amplify it in a manner which I will now describe.

Last year I did some local research on swallow migration and discovered that the first swallows returned to the Santa Monica Mountains on March 20. It would seem reasonable that swallows arriving in San Juan Capistrano on March 19, particularly if they arrived in the evening as Jack Smith's report would suggest, would reach L.A. on the following day. A consideration here is that swallows are among the few songbirds which migrate in the daytime. They are able to do so because their flight is sufficiently swift and erratic for them to elude hawks along the way.

To recapitulate, swallows spending the night at Capistrano and choosing to move on rather than nesting at the Mission, would be expected to arrive in L.A. the next day. And sure enough they did arrive on the expected day.

One problem with my findings was that the birds I saw on March 20 were Rough-winged Swallows, whereas the Mission birds are Cliff Swallows. I think this species difference might be overlooked since most people can't tell the difference between a

Cliff Swallow and a Rough-winged Swallow anyhow. Swallows dart about so rapidly that even most birders can't tell one from another. Furthermore, publicity reports issued by the Capistrano Chamber of Commerce always refer simply to "swallows".

So I think we can establish a foundation for a legend about the swallows returning to the City of Angels on the same day every year. The P.R. people who are responsible for grooming L.A.'s image can make sure that every media mention of the Capistrano swallows includes attention to the Day After, when the swallows would be found to have arrived in our fair town. As the public got used to the association of the legend with L.A. the media might be steered toward alluding to the Capistrano arrival as the Day Before and perhaps eventually dropping the linkage and allowing the newly created L.A. legend to stand on its own two feet.

If our city fathers are interested in promoting this legend, I will be willing to organize an annual survey of swallow migration into the L.A. area to establish the authenticity of the arrival date.

# Mystical Messages

The Canyon Wren's descending song
Cascades down the canyon wall
Stirring a sun-lazy lizard
To a round of stilted pushups.
The pulsating sound flows into a cave
Where a nesting owl turns toward the pulse
And follows the sound down to a field
Where she catches a mouse
And returns to feed her young.
The song reaches out
Like the finger of God,
Triggering the young Adam
For his leap into life.

*Canyon Wren*

*Gerry Haigh*

# A Dance in the Wild

Tall, ramrod straight
he stands in solemn dignity surrounded by space created by the
diffidence of others
re approaching him.
He is suddenly seen to be moving.
At a snail's pace, he lifts one long leg,
extends it and puts it down.
He repeats the same deliberate motions
to reposition his other leg.

Entranced by the elegance of this creature,
I see him as an ambassador to mankind
here to teach us that we may live
with such a degree of grace and tranquility
as we have not even imagined.

While I am admiring his serenity, he suddenly thrusts his bill
like a flash of lightening
into the water beneath him.
He spears a frog which he tosses
into the air above him
and swallows  whole as it falls back.
I learn that even while in meditative repose
one may be fully mindful of one's surroundings.

This stalking heron seems to follow
the yoga of action as taught by Krishna to Arjuna.
Totally focused, he performs with elegance approaching the
sublime,
reminding us perhaps of Barishnikov
but without the countless hours of patience,
or the purpose of impressing an audience.
Does this Great Blue Heron fret when he misses
or does he simply move gracefully on?
I see him as free of attachment to  the consequences of his action.

# The Changing of the Thrushes

Seasonal changes in the wilderness of Los Angeles are relatively subtle, in marked contrast with the glare and gaudiness with which man-made events are staged in our town. The natural world has its spectacles, like earthquakes and volcanoes but most of the changes which occur from day to day go by unnoticed except by the keen observers among us.

The birds, for example, are always in flux, with some moving in and some moving out. One example is the changing of the thrushes whose significance is heightened by the fact that it marks a seasonal change.

This change was heralded for me on a mid-March morning. I had awakened in the still-dark of predawn by the barking of a lonely dog. A single Great Horned Owl was sounding off his last few hoots of the night. The clamorous cacophony of House Finches had not yet begun.

A loud, clear burst of bird song stirred in me memories reaching as far back as boyhood at Grandma's house in the Hudson River Valley. I was hearing the song of the Robin for the first time of the year!

Later in the morning I saw a pair of Robins foraging in our garden. They were staking out their territory in preparation for nesting again at our place. I realized that it had been several days since I had seen the Hermit Thrush which had been wintering here. Although it had been feeding on our grounds since October, I was not to see it again until the coming fall.

The tawny-tailed thrush of winter, the Hermit Thrush, had been replaced by the tawny-breasted thrush, the Robin, of spring. The changing of the thrushes, although occurring annually rather than daily, is as regular and significant an event as the changing of the guard at Buckingham Palace. The latter ceremony, of course, is conducted with much more pomp and fanfare. Nevertheless, the changing of the thrushes is arguably more portentous in that it marks the transition from winter to spring.

## *Robin Not a Robin*

It may come as a surprise to know that our Robin is a thrush. It may be even more surprising to know that our Robin is not truly a Robin. (Was it Mark Twain who said that Shakespeare's plays were not written by Shakespeare at all but by someone else with the same name?)

When our forefathers first settled here, they apparently tried to feel at home in this strange land by seeking similarities with the familiar from which they had come. For starters, they called the new place "New England". One of the birds they found here reminded them of the Robin Redbreast, commonly found both in the English countryside and in European folklore. (The birds which covered with leaves the Babes in the Wood were Robin Redbreasts.) To capture the similarity between the Old World and New World birds, they named the new one "Robin".

When the scientific classifiers got around to sorting out all the avian species in the Americas, they decided that the American Robin and the European Robin Redbreast did not even belong in the same family. Instead, they put our Robin in with the thrushes. The most prominent feature of the thrushes is their speckled breast. The plain-breasted Robin doesn't seem to belong. However, family affinity shows up in young Robins who sport large spots on their breasts. Sentiment won out over science and the Robin was allowed to keep its original name even though some ornithologists fussed over the inaccuracy of it.

The Robin and the Hermit Thrush are both highly esteemed for their voices. The Robin's song is perhaps the best known among all American birds while the Hermit's, although less well known, is one of the most highly prized for its quality.

*Sweep of Singing Birds*

The Robin's song heralds the arrival of spring thaw, as the wave of singing birds sweeps up the continent from southern Mexico to northern Canada, advancing as the nighttime temperatures go above freezing.

Once they arrive at any given latitude, the dawning of each spring day is celebrated as "a wave of Robin song rises on the Atlantic coast ... and, preceding the rising sun, rolls across the land until at last it breaks and dies away upon the ... shores of the Pacific Ocean." (Forbush, 1925)

In contrast with the ubiquitous nature of Robin-song, few people know the song of the Hermit Thrush. Even Audubon apparently never knew it. While the bird is wintering with us in the Santa Monica Mountains, the only sound it makes is a one-note "chuck" call. However, when the Hermit reaches its nesting grounds in the Sierra and beyond, it gives voice to a song which some connoisseurs consider to be even more beautiful than that of the Nightingale, the

European thrush which has long been celebrated in literature as the finest avian singer in the world.

Walt Whitman wrote of the Hermit Thrush: "Having studied the mockingbirds tones and the flight of the mountain hawk, I heard at dawn the unrivaled one, the hermit thrush from the swamp cedars."

The effect on the listener of the Hermit's song has been described by the great naturalist, John Burroughs: "Mounting toward the upland again, I pause reverently as the hush and stillness of twilight comes upon the woods. It is the sweetest, ripest hour of the day. And as the Hermit's evening hymn goes up from the deep solitude below me, I experience that serene exaltation of sentiment of which music, literature and religion are but the faint types and symbols."

It is indeed worth listening for this song if you are hiking in the Sierra in late spring or early summer. When you hear musical notes pealing forth from deep within a coniferous forest and you feel tingles running up and down your spine, you will know that you are probably listening to a Hermit Thrush.

## Contrast in Temperament

The two thrushes contrast markedly in temperament. The Hermit is shy and solitary. The Robin is bold and gregarious. Thus, most sightings of the Hermit during winter around L.A. are of single birds feeding in the shadows on the ground. The Robin, on the other hand, except when nesting, usually travels in flocks of at least ten and sometimes up to thousands foraging in the Santa Monica Mountains.

Also, while the Hermit's nest is secreted within coniferous forests and is seldom found by people, the Robin often builds its nest in conspicuous places near our dwellings. And in regard to feeding, who has not seen Robins searching for earthworms wherever there are lawns, but how many of us have ever seen the Hermit sorting among forest leaves for berries and insects?

When the changing of the thrushes occurs with the advent of spring, it is consistent with their contrasting lifestyles that many will notice the arrival of the Robin and few will note the departure of the Hermit.

*Hermit Thrush*

# The Hepatic Factor

Some friends we were visiting in Ontario, California, told us they were shown a Hepatic Tanager the day before. I had never heard of a Hepatic Tanager and since these friends were not "real birders", I was inclined to dismiss their report.

On second thought, I recalled an experience I had had during my first week in Topanga. I was in Herb Gutman's backyard and we heard a bird he called a Wrentit that I had never heard of before. I rashly declared that there was no such bird as a Wrentit. I went on to explain that there were wrens and there were tits. Since there were no tits this side of Europe, the bird must be some kind of wren.

True enough there was no such bird in New York where I had come from, but when I looked it up in my Western Field Guide at home, I discovered that there was a genuine bird in the southwest called a Wrentit. So I had to call Herb and eat crow. But it was worth it. I could add a new bird to my life list.

Getting back to the Hepatic Tanager, not only had I never heard of the bird, I also had never heard of the word 'Hepatic'. My only association was to hepatitis, a disease. I searched the dictionary and discovered that "hepatic" had something to do with the liver, either its shape or its color. I cautiously ruled out shape since I was fairly confident that the bird in question was probably not shaped like a liver so it must be colored like a liver.

Though I didn't have my field guide with me to check if there was such a bird, I asked them to find it again and show it to me. The odds are slim for finding a bird in the same place it was the day before, so I wasn't optimistic when my friend John took us to the very tree on which they had seen it. But lo! Not only was it on the same tree but it was also feeding in the same part of the tree! I not only had a new life bird but I added a new color to my visual vocabulary.

Within a week I had another experience with the hepatic color. I was standing on the shore of a little pool in our box canyon where months before I had dropped in a dozen tiny goldfish. I thought they had all been washed downstream or swallowed up by marauding raccoons. Then, one day, I was surprised and delighted to discover a six-inch goldfish swimming idly near the top. The sun was shining down so that it projected a dark shadow on the bottom of the pool. I was watching this interplay between the fish, his shadow and the sun when suddenly the shadow took off in a different direction!

It took me a moment to recover from the shock until I realized that it wasn't a shadow but a different fish. Peering intently at it I saw that it was the same hepatic color as the new Tanager in my life.

When I realized I was dealing not with a fish and its shadow but with two separate fish, I became interested in the relationship between the two. I saw that the goldfish was always suspended within an inch or two of the top of the pool while the hepatic fish always stayed within an inch or two of the bottom. Since the pool is only eight to ten inches deep, this meant they were often close to each other. I assumed they were mates and that the brightly colored one was the male as is usual in the animal kingdom. Why was the male always above the female? Could it be a matter of dominance or hierarchy? Could it be a matter of chivalry, with the male assuming the more vulnerable position in the event of attack? (Males are more expendable for the continuation of the species and are therefore allowed to be more noticeable to predators.)

The problem reminds me of a piece of doggerel about frogs:

Two green frogs sitting on a leaf.
One is a wife the other is the chief.
She knows that no one can tell them apart.
She won't let him know.
It might break his heart.

The doggerel is, of course irrelevant for the problem at hand Some problems in nature are very difficult to understand even for people of considerable wisdom. So let us drop this problem with no shame.

# Hidden Crowns

Spring is at its peak in Topanga, a time for bright colors in the plant world, the human world, the bird world. There are two birds here now which are occasionally displaying bright crowns, i.e., they part head feathers which ordinarily conceal the patches otherwise hidden the rest of the year.

One is the Ruby-crowned Kinglet, an olive-gray bird about the size of a Bushtit (very small). It has a broken white eye-ring, which makes its eye look large, and it repeatedly shakes its shoulders excitedly as it feeds in the trees. The crown is the color of a Scarlet Penstemmon, in bloom now.

The other bird is the Orange-crowned Warbler, a dull yellow-green bird (about the size of a House Finch), which is currently singing its colorless trill in chaparral and live oak throughout Topanga. Its crown is the color of a Monkey Flower.

The Kinglet is curious about people and can easily be lured into close view by making swishing sounds with your mouth. The Warbler is very elusive. These days I can step into my backyard and hear two or three of them singing, but I have not actually seen one since the Christmas bird census this past winter. (The Audubon Society conducts an annual census of birds throughout North America during Christmas week.) The Kinglets winter here and in another month will leave for the mountains to nest, some near the top of Mt. Pinos.

The Warblers winter between here and Guatemala. At this time of year, a lot of migrants are passing through Topanga, small numbers of which will stay here to breed.

The Ruby-crowned Kinlet and the Orange-crowned Warbler are both drab birds which have the distinction of being able to display a bright burst of color. The Penstemmon and the Monkey Flower (indeed, all of our wildflowers) are similarly drab except for seasonal displays of bright color. All of these eruptions of color, avian and floral, play a part in the regeneration of life, and among the more subtle splendors celebrating this regeneration is the revealing of the otherwise hidden crowns of the Kinglet and the Warbler.

# The Return of Spring

Earth is emerging
from the death of winter
into the vernal mysteries
of renewal and rebirth.
Walking through a cryptic grove of oak,
I see a thousand tiny tubes of blood
dangling everywhere in the shadows
of dark green leaves.
I hear the dying scream
of a woodland rat
swooped off the forest floor
by a fierce female raptor.
Her mate awaits nearby.
Tamed by the mating urge,
he purrs like a kitten.
A black and gray vulture,
undertaker of the wild,
soars effortlessly overhead
in overlapping circles
seeking out the scent
of death and dying.

I leave the darkened grove
and enter a sunlit meadow.

Wild lilac fills the air
with its heady perfume.
Patches of blue larkspur
and golden buttercups

adorn the fresh green grass.
An Orange-tip butterfly
hovers over his mate.
Perched on Purple Sage,
she is waiting to receive him
with her wings spread in the sun.

Yes, spring is here again,
celebrating the wondrous cycle
of death and resurrection.

# Wave of Warblers and Birders
# Floods Topanga Park

Richard Kahlenberg, a Journalist for the LA Times, wrote an article about my bird walks at Trippet Ranch. It appeared on a Friday before the Sunday saunter and, such is the power of the press, instead of the usual dozen, forty-five people showed up to look for birds and most of them first-timers! Also, most of them were from the Valley because, as it turned out, the article was printed only in the Valley edition.

Near the beginning of the jaunt, we saw a spectacular drama focused on a Red-tailed Hawk perched atop a utility pole. It was being dive bombed alternately by a Kestrel and a Crow. The Kestrel was a male in beautiful blue, red, black and white plumage. This, our smallest falcon, was diving from an altitude of about seventy feet above the pole. On the way down, he twisted and turned splendidly until he reached the head of the hawk which he seemed to graze as he turned upward. Then he ascended, also twisting and turning, hovered for a moment, then dove again.

The Crow was attacking in a much more pedestrian mode from about ten feet up and never pulling out closer than two feet from the raptor. He must have been depending more upon vocal noise to frighten because as he dove he was 'crowing' coarsely, as only crows can do! After about a half dozen dives of the falcon, the big Buteo hawk pushed off from the pole and flew leisurely away.

Another dramatic event occurred toward the end of our hike. As we approached the dirt bank where trap-door spiders hang out, we discovered that the oak grove behind the bank was alive with birds! Hundreds of them were alternately flitting or feeding from branch to branch. The main constituents of the flock were three species of warbler, namely: Black-throated Gray, Townsend's, and MacGillivray's. We also saw three other warblers during the morning: Common Yellowthroat, Virginia's and Hermit.

This was a red letter day for warblers for the regulars among us. The number of species and the size of the group were unusually high. We recognized them as migrants who had probably dropped in near dawn after having flown three or four hundred miles thru the night. The birds had come from the boreal belt across our Northern states and Canada or from the high Sierras. By sunset they will take off again for Central and South America.

It has been several years since we have seen that large and varied a flock of warblers passing through Topanga. Warblers throughout the Western Hemisphere have been decreasing rapidly in recent years. Two major factors have been identified as responsible for the decrease. One is the decrease in their wintering grounds. Fully half of the world's rain forests have been destroyed. The other major reason is that their nesting grounds throughout the United States have become alarmingly fragmented which brings many problems for nesting birds including increased pressure from nest predators such as raccoons, crows and jays which prowl the edges while avoiding deep penetration. Fragments are also more frequently parasitized by Cowbirds and by cats. Topangans have been carrying on a moderately successful fight against fragmentation as witness our new park instead of a development in Summit Valley.

In summary, we were happy to treat our new birder friends from the valley to forty-nine species of birds with particular emphases on the six species of warbler! Thank you Richard Kahlenberg for having inspired them to join our saunter. And thank you birds for turning out in such numbers.

*Crow*

# Ocean Wanderers

At five thirty in the morning, I am standing at the bow of a boat moving thru a thick fog with a maximum visibility of twenty feet, body pulled back from the cold wind and spray, my eyes peering forward into the fog.

I boarded the Paisano late last night when it was tied up at the dock in Oxnard. Some friends and I threw sleeping bags on the deck and slept until the engine started up at four thirty. At five, we left port and headed for the Channel Islands.

Now, half an hour out of Oxnard, nearly sightless in the fog, nearly frigid in the cold, struggling to keep my balance on a rolling, pitching deck, with a faint taste of nausea in my mouth, I ask myself; "What an I doing here?"

Suddenly a dark blob rises from the water and assumes the form of a bird just before it disappears into the fog. "Sooty Shearwater" cries out the man beside me and a day of birding has begun. Discomforts are quickly forgotten as the fog gradually lifts and the ocean becomes alive with birds, porpoises, fish.

We saw many kinds of birds that day but none so numerous

as the Sooty Shearwater. We saw the Sootys going by in flocks containing hundreds of thousands of birds, leading us to estimate that there must be many millions of them in our waters, making them probably the most abundant bird in California that day. There were also small flocks alternately feeding and resting on the water. When a Shearwater would take off from the water at the approach of our boat, we had a chance to see how the first birds may have learned to fly 150 million years ago. They run along the water with their narrow wings outstretched until they reach the critical speed at which lift overcomes gravity and they plane into the air. Was it in some similar manner that Archaeopteryx raced over the ground in pursuit of insects, with his feathered arms thrust rigidly out to serve as a net, and suddenly found himself soaring instead of running, and thus became the first bird to fly?

Once airborne, the Shearwater characteristically flaps a few times then goes into a long glide close to the water on rigid down-curved wings, tilting and wheeling, then flapping again. It sometimes shears off the tips of the waves, from which action it gets its name.

As I marveled at the flight of the Sooty Shearwater, I wondered where they had come from, where they were going, what was their story? While most birds migrating through California in the spring are heading toward their nesting grounds, I learned that the Shearwaters are not. Instead, the Sooty nests during our wintertime at the bottom of the world, on islands between the Straits of Magellan and Antarctica. When the brief south polar summer ends, the Shearwaters leave in large flocks. One flock was observed which contained over 150 million birds. They go up both sides of the South American continent, some traversing the Atlantic as far as Greenland, the rest traversing the Pacific as far as Alaska. Those birds which reach the limit or their range will have made a round trip of twenty-two thousand miles.

How they find their way over such vast distances is still a mystery to man. An experiment was performed with a Manx Shearwater in which a female tending her half-grown young one was taken from her nesting burrow in Wales and flown by jet to Boston where she was released. She was back with her nestling twelve days later, having flown three thousand miles by what had to be the shortest possible route considering the time elapsed. What makes this feat even more remarkable is that the Manx Shearwater normally migrates between Europe and Africa so that the journey from Boston to Wales was over unknown waters and at right angles to its usual pathways.

Ever since man has been trying to find his own way across the vast seas of our planet, we have probably felt a deep respect for those pelagic birds which navigate these same routes so surely. A sacred chant of ancient Polynesian navigators illustrates this feeling:

"Mine is the migrating bird
winging over perilous regions of the ocean,
ever tracing out the age-old path
of the wandering waves ...."

My migrating birds this day were the Sooty Shearwaters. We met somewhere between Oxnard and Anacapa, while I was on a round trip between Topanga and Santa Barbara Island. And they were on a round trip between Antarctica and Alaska. I don't know how they felt about me, or if they even noticed me, but I felt great admiration and respect for them.

*Egret*

# Predictability in the Wild

Critics of our culture tell us that mankind is getting farther and farther away from our roots. While many philosophers agree with Thoreau that in wildness lies the preservation of the world, we see more and more people in the world becoming urbanized and suburbanized and increasingly distanced from nature.

One easy remedy for Angelenos who yearn for more contact with wild things is to get out for nature walks sponsored throughout the Santa Monica Mountains. There we can gain some sense of tranquility in observing the simple, predictable behavior of wild

82

creatures, such as our feathered friends. We can watch the Towhees which are usually scratching in the dirt. We can see the doves rising from the ground on whistling wings and darting through the air in their customary way. We can observe the hawk which perches on the same utility pole every morning waiting for the air to warm up sufficiently to support his soaring body.

In our quest for orderliness and predictability, it may be disconcerting to find some birds doing strange things. For example, last spring some kind-hearted people were upset at witnessing two small birds frantically foraging to feed a monstrous baby bird almost twice as big as they were. Baby was squawking out its demands almost continuously and every few minutes momma or poppa would return to drop food into its gaping maw.

The folks were even more horrified when they learned that the ravenous juvenile was a Cowbird who had evicted the proper offspring from the nest of its adopted parents. Thus the adult warblers were driven to appease the enormous hunger of the baby which had been dumped into their lives. I am sure that parents of demanding teenagers may see some parallels in human society.

It may also be disturbing to find birds out of place. One comes to rely upon the propensity of wild creatures to abide each in its own proper habitat. We don't expect to find hummingbirds swimming in the pond or to find ducks hovering over flowers. Incongruities of that kind are apt to be upsetting.

During a recent bird walk, our attention was drawn at one point to the top of an oak tree where some four or five Titmouses were making a loud racket. Their alarm cries were so loud and shrill that we guessed they must be threatened by some predator. A Great Horned Owl, a Cooper's Hawk or even a bobcat came to mind as possibilities. We were startled to discover a Roadrunner perched in the treetop and stirring up the ruckus. Everybody knows that Roadrunners are so named because they run along the road or at least on the ground which they use as a road. Rarely will they perch in a low bush within five or six feet of the ground. What was this one doing high in a tree? Did he think he was raptor and was he trying to catch smaller birds?

On another bird walk, we encountered another incongruity. We were standing on the bluff overlooking Santa Ynez Canyon. (It also overlooks a housing development but naturalists tend to avoid noticing such blights upon the landscape.) This is a favorite lookout for observing soaring vultures, raptors and ravens. Someone spotted two white patches on the ridge line of the mountain between us and the ocean. We lifted our binoculars and discovered two Great Egrets standing in the top of a tree. Egrets are herons and herons hang out around the water. The closest place we'd seen egrets before was at the Malibu Lagoon. What were these egrets doing on a mountaintop?

We were puzzling over this question when the birds spread their wings and leaped into the air. They flapped a few times, caught a thermal and began to soar. They went round and round in wide circles, rising higher, dropping lower, floating on the warm air without flapping a wing. They were riding the thermals exactly the same way as do the vultures, the eagles and the hawks.

It is quite understandable for raptors to soar like that. They are scanning wide tracts of the ground below for prey. But the egret forages for its food by stalking slowly with its feet in the water and with its bill and long neck poised to strike.

What were these egrets doing soaring high in the sky? Were they trying it out just for kicks? Had they gotten onto this sport by watching the raptors and the ravens?

Until our experience that Sunday morning, I would have told you that there is about as much chance to see an egret catching the high thermals as there is to see a duck hovering in front of honey-suckle flowers. Now I feel unsettled. The wild has lost some of its predictability for me. Could that be a hummingbird I see swimming in my birdbath?

# The Lone Kingfisher of Topanga Creek

Early every morning I see a bird perched on a wire over the road halfway down the S-curves. His silhouette is unique. About the size of a Scrub Jay (a.k.a. Blue Jay), he has a big head and bill and small feet and tail. He sports an outrageous crest, which must look to some like a Crown because he is called king.

From his perch on the wire, he looks out over Topanga Creek. His interest is not so much aesthetic as predatory, for he is a fisher by trade. His crest and his trade are both honored in his full name of Kingfisher.

When he deems it time to feed, the Kingfisher will drop down to the creek and patrol it, flying beneath the treetops, giving his wild rattling call. Sometimes he perches on a limb, sometimes he hovers over the stream. When he spots a fish, he dives straight down into the water and spears it with his bill. Then he flies to a branch and beats the fish senseless, tosses it up into the air, catches it head first and swallows it.

It is not by chance that there is but one Kingfisher on the wire for this bird is a loner. Having staked out a length of stream for himself, he will chase any other Kingfisher away. He becomes sociable for the sake of raising a family. For that, he teams up with a mate and the pair will work hard together to dig out a burrow in a bank which may be as deep as fifteen feet, more or less straight in. The female incubates the eggs for about twenty-four days, all during which period she is fed by the male. When the eggs hatch, there may be between five and fourteen young to be fed. They work arduously at this task until the young are able to fly. Then, their last demanding task is to teach their offspring how to fish.

Fishing school is tutorial in nature. A parent perches over a stream beside one of his young'uns. When the adult spots a fish, he dives down, spears it, brings it back up to the branch where the youngster expectantly opens wide his mouth. However, the parent, after killing the fish by beating it against the branch, drops it down into the stream. The pupil quickly learns that he can appease his hunger only by catching fish himself and within a week is catching live ones.

As soon as their offspring learn to fend for themselves, the parents drive them away, separate from each other, and return to their loner lifestyle.

Exhausted by the demands of raising a family, the Kingfisher, alone on the wire, like the drunk in the midnight choir, or the balloon rising higher and higher, tries in his way to be free.

*Kingfisher*

# Phainopepla:  Black Prince of the Wild

I am sitting against a cliff in the shade when I hear the sweet, familiar call, "pretty boy." This brings to my mind the name "Phain-opepla" and the image of a wondrously handsome bird, — slim and trim with iridescent black plumage and a proud crest

I follow the call to the top of a nearby pine which is very tall, very dead and very black from the '93 fire. At the topmost tip of the tree is a small black spot.

Leaning back against the cliff, I raise my binoculars and make out the tiny silhouette of a bird with barely discernible crest, hardly a replica of the handsome image in my mind but enough clues to call it a Phainopepla. The name is derived from two Greek words which, together, mean "shiny robe," an appropriately descriptive term.

The tiny dot didn't hold my attention long, so I shifted to the meadow and the tree. There, a White-tailed Kite was just slipping over the horizon with indolent grace.  As the Kite glided away a playful breeze sprang up and set all into motion, drawing attention to everything except to itself.

Then, on the ground in front of me, a little mouse creature in soft grey fur took advantage of all the wind-driven motion which would prevent his own movements from standing out. He scurried to the shelter of some large grey boulders and disappeared from sight. A two-ribboned garter snake slinked smoothly along the crevices between the rocks. Suddenly the mouse reappeared and jumped over the snake, whereupon they both disappeared into separate holes in the ground.

The dance of the rodent and the serpent was sensual, subtle and silent but it was eerily apparent that the stakes might be life and death.

My eyes were drawn to the top of the pine again where a second bird darted into view. The two began chasing, playing tag in three dimensional space. When they flew close enough, I saw that they were both male Phainopepla. They raised their wings above their heads on every stroke, making their flight look fluttery, much like a butterfly. Flying exposes white patches on their wings, creating a striking effect against the glossy black.

I was reminded of an incident illustrating the survival value of these white patches. Since the Phaino customarily perches at the top of bushes or trees, it often presents a tempting target to raptors on the hunt. I once observed one in this vulnerable position under attack by that assassin of the wild, a Cooper's Hawk. Just as the hawk was about to grab its meal, the Phaino raised its wings and sprang into the air. The predator was suddenly confronted with a dazzling white distraction which disrupted its attack, leaving it with a few feathers instead of the body of its intended victim and the Phaino flew away.

When the two males finished their game of tag, they dropped out of sight in the chaparral around me. They began uttering a soft "yerp" call which soon attracted a third bird which flew across my field of view. It looked identical to the others, except that instead of smashing black it was drab grey. It was, of course, a female, which gender in the bird world is almost universally plain in contrast with the colorful males.

The males obviously did not share my disparaging view of the female's attractiveness, because they immediately rose into the air and began cavorting with her. Whereas their flight had previously been playful and erratic, it now became focused and erotic. Although the males were each courting the female, they did not seem competitive with each other. I suddenly realized that I was witnessing a sylvan ménage a trois. Frequently in Phainopeplas, two males and a female will bond with each other to build a nest and raise a family.

Not since the happy hippie Sixties have I seen this pattern in our species. The politically correct view of family values in today's world would hardly allow such an arrangement to be considered wholesome.

However idiosyncratic the family life of Phainopeplas, they seem to be deeply invested in it. They are the only bird species which routinely raises two families a year in two entirely different habitats. In January and February they nest in the deserts of Southern California and neighboring states. In June and July they come up-mountain and nest again in the chaparral country like Topanga.

What led to the development of this fascinating Phaino migratory pattern? Food supply is always a major factor in the movement of birds, and birds are most dependent on an ample food supply during breeding season. The Phainopepla finds a major source of sustenance in the berries of the Mistletoe plant. Their stay in the Sonoran desert coincides with maximum production of Mistletoe berries on the Mesquite trees there. While they are breeding in the Santa Monicas, Mistletoe berries are most abundant in our Coast Live Oak trees.

Along with berries, the other major staple in the Phaino diet is insects, which they usually catch in the air. While foraging for berries is hardly facilitated by perching at the tops of trees, catching insects decidedly is. Thus, their perch on high is probably not used for posing, but as a lookout and springboard for leaping into the air and sallying forth to snatch up insects. They often return to the perch in the manner of flycatchers. In fact, another name for the Phainopepla is Shiny Flycatcher.

This flycatcher with the shiny robe is one of the most fascinating birds who share the Topanga habitat with us. While they are most abundant during the summer, there are always a few which stay with us year 'round.

# Family Values

I was walking on the Musch trail
when a slight movement in a bush
caught my eye.
After a moment, a small brown bird
came into view.
His gray head and long jaunty tail
identified him as a Wrentit,
so often heard but so seldom seen.
I enjoyed a long, leisurely look
until he slipped out of sight again.
Another bird feeding in the brush nearby
caught my attention.
I wondered what it was
until suddenly I remembered:
Wrentits are always in pairs-
feeding, sleeping, nesting-
they live lives totally committed
to each other.

A few yards farther along,
I spotted another pair of birds
feeding together in the brush.
They were Brown Towhees,
which also mate for life
and live lives fully committed
to each other.
I drifted out of the woodland
wondering how many
of our fellow beings
in the universe
act out life-long commitments
to a mate.

*Anna's Hummingbird*

# Wrentit and Hummingbird: A Study in Values

Early this year, I walked one day through meadows in the Santa Monica Mountains. The plants were many shades of brown and gray with only an occasional bit of color supplied by the lovely violet blossoms of a few Brodiea hidden low down in the grasses. Spring, which usually arrives with the rains, had not yet arrived in our drought-ridden L.A. wilderness.

I stopped to rest under a Live Oak, took off my shoes and socks and picked 207 seeds off one sock and about the same number off the other. As I plucked, my mind emptied and I became aware of the stillness around me. There was no sound, no movement. The world was at peace. I was at peace.

Suddenly, very close to my left ear, a male Wrentit burst into his loud, clear, ping-pong song. He sang out five times in close sequence and then the world around me lapsed back into silence. Though I usually hear Wrentits singing in the chaparral any time of day and any time of year, this particular Wrentit song was the most beautiful I had ever heard. The simple repetitive task of pulling seeds from a sock had prepared my mind to receive his music. I had been able to shed the contrived social world of Man and be simply there, in the wild.

These are the moments which bring the fisherman back again and again to the stream; the mountaineer back to the mountain; the birder back to the brush. As I drifted away from my absorption in the moment, I began thinking about the Wrentit in general. Like the Anna's Hummingbird, found only in California and Southern Arizona, the Wrentit does not migrate. Both species are with us year round, and very few of either are found beyond the boundaries of our state.

The differences between our two year-round birds are enormous. The Wrentit is so drab and reclusive that most Angelenos do not even know it exists. Like the grasses in the meadow, Wrentits are colored brown and gray, allowing them to blend with brush in which they spend most of their lives.

In contrast the male Anna is the showiest bird in Southern California. Is there a single Angeleno who has not at some time been dazzled by the brilliant color flashing from its throat and crown? Even the less colorful female is familiar to us because hummers frequent our gardens and feeders and are so fearless that they are apt, at any time, to approach as close as inches from our face.

In getting around, the Wrentit moves mostly with its legs while the hummer moves only with its wings. The Wrentit can run through a tangle of branches faster than a man can run across open ground. It takes to the air only occasionally to cross a trail from one patch of shrubbery to another. On these short flights, it looks awkward, pumping its tail in a clumsy manner.

The hummer on the other hand does not even walk, let alone run, but is the most versatile flyer in the world. It can fly straight up, straight down, sideways, backwards, forwards, or hover in one place. To execute these maneuvers, it must beat its wings as much as eighty times in one second.

The comparative prominence of these birds reverses itself when we shift from the visual to the auditory world. The song of the Wrentit has been heard by millions of people all over the world. This is so because it is the frequently occurring birdsong on the soundtrack of Hollywood movies. This notoriety does not intrude upon the Wrentits anonymity, because audiences rarely identify the bird singing in the distance while the cowboy lopes along on his horse in the foreground.

Hummers, in contrast, have such a faint squeaky voice that it barely merits being called a song, and what they do utter can only be heard at fairly close range. In summary, we can say that hummers are usually seen but not heard, whereas Wrentits are usually heard but not seen.

The differences in lifestyles between the males of these two species are of such a dramatic nature as to make anthropomorphizing irresistible to this (male) writer.

The Wrentit is a model mate, exemplifying the best of family-oriented middle-class values. Dependable and committed, he mates for life. A paragon of stability, he spends his entire life on a two-acre parcel of land. Intimate and attentive, he forms an intense bond with his mate. Day in and day out, he forages with her, keeping consistently within calling distance. (If you happen to see one Wrentit, there will probably be another nearby.)

He shares the work of building the nest and raising the young.

*Wrentit*

96

Some nights he sleeps with her with feathers intertwined, inner legs interlocked, heads pressed together, so that the pair look like one round ball on two legs.

Everything the male Wrentit is, the male hummer is not. Essentially, he is an irresponsible philanderer. He bonds with his mate for only as long as it takes to woo her. His courting is spectacular. He flashes his dazzling red throat and crown to attract her attention. When he has it, he spirals up into the sky until he is almost out of sight (to us). He then dives at tremendous speed almost straight down, bottoms out just above where she is perched, and gives vent to a loud "wonk" noise. He hovers above her for a few seconds and then flies to a nearby perch and repeats the entire performance.

Once the female succumbs to this dashing display, she will have only a brief moment with her consort. They will fly up into the air and copulate within a few seconds. Then the female goes off alone to build a nest, lay eggs, incubate, and raise the young on her own.

The moral lesson which arises in this comparison between these males is confusing. Judged by our usual social standards, the Wrentit comes through as an admirable fellow—though his zeal to please may seem excessive to some. The shallow, flashy hummer merits disparagement, though many men must secretly envy his ability to get away with it. One wonders that any female would allow herself to be taken in by such a bounder, and yet hummingbirds reproduce themselves every year just as surely as do Wrentits.

These philosophical musings are reduced to whimsy by the fact that bird behavior is minimally influenced by avian social values, and predominantly determined by DNA driven instincts.

We humans are left to wonder at the diversity of adaptive patterns which birds have evolved.

We may also wonder where the human males we know fall on the scale between "Hummingbirdness and Wrentitness".

# Male Dominance

The most vicious attack I have ever seen by a male hummer was against a very weak female. She had somehow gotten trapped in our house overnight. I discovered her in the morning flying feebly between the rafters in our high-ceilinged living room. I worked her down with a long bamboo frond, caught her at a window and released her in our backyard.

She flew to a feeder and was immediately attacked by a male who drove her down to the floor of the deck where he jumped on her back and began whipping her with the side of his bill. After a few minutes of this assault, which was endured completely passively by the female, he flew off and perched nearby. She lay pressed against the deck for a few moments then rose and flew weakly to the feeder. Before she could feed, the male attacked again, knocking the female backwards from the perch but she hung on with her feet. The male seized the female by the ankles with his own feet and flew off with her to a nearby bush. They both lit in the center of the bush and the male began battering the female with his wings and with his beak. The female fell over backwards again and was hanging onto a branch upside down. The male flew away.

I tried to catch the female but she flew away before my hand touched her. She flew towards the feeder with a feeble fluttering flight. The male attacked again in midair. She lit on a cloth bag and clung there while the male clung to her back, again battering away at her. After a moment she lost her grip and fell to the deck. Again, he pounced on her back and began bill-whipping her. I ran up to the second floor of my house, got my camera, loaded it and ran back. When I returned, he still had her pinned down to the deck. As I came out the door, he picked her up in his feet and flew off with her, disappearing through some trees about one hundred feet away.

An editor for the Audubon Magazine noted that hummers are well known to be territorial creatures. They will drive away hawk moths, butterflies, other hummers and even bees; anything that competes for the nectar supply. Laboratory studies have shown hummers passing a large percentage of their body weight daily in the form of bodily waste fluids. Hummers will adjust the size of their territory until they have the maximum food available with the minimum effort.

# Why Women Prefer Penguins
# to Hummingbirds

Frantically foraging and feeding, two small birds were enslaved by a monster baby bird almost twice as big as they were. Baby was squawking out its demands almost continuously and every few minutes mama or papa would return to drop food into its gaping maw.

My friend Eric had discovered this bizarre trio in the oak grove by the pond at Trippet Ranch during our monthly bird walk. He directed my attention to the drama being enacted high in the Coast Live Oaks just below the canopy.

The two small birds were slim, handsome adults. They were blue-gray above and white below, had white eye rings and long black and white tails.

While they were like wrens in having the same busy way of feeding, were similar in size, and occasionally cocked their tails straight up, these were definitely not wrens. These harried and hapless victims were Bluegray Gnatcatchers.

Gnatcatchers spend much of the year in Central America and fly up to the USA to nest and raise their young. A hazard they face in trying to accomplish this task is that they are one of the species of small birds which are frequently parasitized by the Cowbird.

The big fat juvenile these two Gnatcatchers were so busily feeding was a Cowbird. Its mother had deposited it inside an eggshell in the Gnatcatcher nest. Because its incubation period was faster, the young Cowbird quickly outstripped in size its Gnatcatcher siblings. When it got big enough, it muscled them out of the nest to die on the ground below. Such is the struggle for survival in the natural world, even in Topanga State Park.

Now, instead of raising five young of their own, the parent Gnatcatchers were faced with the problem of what to do with this one big, ugly stranger. It would seem as if they might have the choice to abandon it and start over again. But do they?

Some host birds have the wisdom to discriminate a Cowbird egg when it is first laid in their nest and they throw it out. Some have apparently not mastered the technical skill to remove one bad egg from a clutch of several eggs and solve the problem by building another floor over the first set of eggs and lay another clutch. (I have found a Yellow Warbler nest which had four levels, each of the lower three having one Cowbird and the fourth with none.)

*Bluegray Gnatcatcher*

Once the eggs hatch, however, the host parents seem to be unable to turn away from a baby begging for food. However ugly a baby cowbird may appear to us and however unlike in appearance it may be to their own species, the victimized parents feed, feed, feed as long as the youngster demands, demands, demands. And the juvenile cowbird continues to demand until it is almost twice the size of its foster parents and goes off to join other cowbirds and feed on its own.

Surely it was not a choiceful decision for these two harried little Gnatcatchers to extend their ongoing hospitality to the uninvited guest who dropped in for dinner and stayed on, killing all of their own family so that he could get all the food for himself! It seems more likely that their willingness to nurture this unattractive and ungracious stranger must derive from a parental instinct so powerful as to override all rational considerations.

In strong contrast to the apparent strength of parental instinct in the Gnatcatchers was almost the lack of any in the 'mother' Cowbird. The only mothering she did was to select a suitable family with which to abandon her offspring.

Such a weak parental instinct is rare among female birds. Only the Cowbird on this continent and the Cuckoo in Europe exhibit this trait. However, weak parental instinct is not uncommon among male birds. Our free-spirited male hummingbirds, for example, give only their sperm to the child rearing process. After attracting a female through spectacular displays of flashing colors and daring flights, the male copulates and moves on. The female is on her own to build a nest, incubate the eggs and feed the young.

All of these patterns of parenting are found among humans. There are mothers who give up their babies for adoption though it is usually done through negotiation rather than dumping on the doorstep. Many couples are as willing as Gnatcatchers to raise someone else's child. Many men move on like hummingbirds leaving young children behind to be raised solely by the mother. We tend to think of these various behaviors as matters of choice, but is it possible that they also are partly determined by differences among us in the strength of the parental instinct?

My wife, Lynne, is very fascinated with the fathering instinct of the Emperor Penguin. She loves to tell the story of how these penguins start their family in the middle of winter in Antarctica. They go inland a few miles where the female lays one egg and returns to the sea to feed. Her mate takes over the egg, puts it in a brood patch near his feet and incubates it for two months. He stands there in the dark with thousands of other males through the Antarctic winter. The temperature is below zero, the winds howl, and the snow flies. Finally, the female returns just as the egg hatches and frees the male to eat again for the first time in two months. However by this time there are forty or fifty miles of ice between him and the ocean which he must cross to reach his food supply.

I am not sure why this story is so appealing to women. I suppose if given a choice among the various parental patterns exemplified by male birds, I can understand that most women would like their mate to be more like an Emperor Penguin than like a Hummingbird.

# I Saved a Hummingbird's Life Once!

Donna's story as told to the Birdman of Topanga.

A mother hummer built a nest once over our back deck. She made it entirely of spider webs! Imagine how much patience it must have taken to find enough webs to build a whole nest. And the whole job had to be done by the female because the male doesn't help one little bit.

When she got finished, I couldn't see into it because it was too close to the roof. So I got a shaving mirror and peeked in every morning. One day, pretty soon, there was one egg in the nest. A few days later the mother started sitting on the nest and I couldn't see in. I kept coming back all day to see if she was still there. Finally, she wasn't on the nest and I discovered that there were two eggs. They were real tiny, but the nest was real tiny too, and they filled it all up.

I stopped visiting the nest for a while because I knew that the mother had to incubate the eggs to make them hatch. So I didn't bother looking any more until the mother started making lots of trips to the nest. That's how I knew the eggs must have hatched and sure enough when I held up the mirror again, there were two tiny naked babies there. I checked them every day and every day you could see that they were bigger than the day before.

One day, after the baby hummers were pretty well grown up, a pair of house finches came to our deck and started to build a nest at the other end. Just then we went away for the weekend. When we came back, we discovered that disaster had struck for the hummers. Their whole nest was torn up and we could see where the finches had ripped it apart and used the webs for their own nest. There was only one baby hummer left and he was hanging by one foot upside down. But he was still alive!

So I loosened up his foot and made a new nest for him out of a tiny toy teacup. I lined it with the spider webs that were left and added some woolen threads I had.

At first I put my nest with the baby in it three inches from where the old nest had been, hoping that the mother would feed it, but she never came back. So I took over and fed it myself.

I fed it every half-hour with a toothpick on which I put a tip of cotton which I dipped in sugar water. The chick had lots of energy and would usually leap up to eat.

I kept that bird for two days including one work day. Then I didn't want to lose any more work days so I took it to a place called the California Wildlife Center. It was just a regular house but full of bird cages. They put my hummer in an incubator. After a week they decided it was ready to fly so they released it in a meadow with a lot of flowers. They said it went right to the blossoms and began feeding itself so it was right at home.

I am proud that I saved that hummingbird!

What do you think I did with the house finches that tore apart the hummers' nest? At first I thought I would tear their nest apart, like they did to the hummer. But I decided that I didn't want to hurt them.

They just didn't know any better. But they got punished anyhow. We had a late rain, and since the finches built their nest in a rain gutter, it got washed out. That also happened to a nest they made a month before. In fact, last year they also lost two of their nests in the rain gutter. You'd think they would learn. But maybe they were always different finches. We have lots of finches in Topanga and they all look alike. I guess a lot of them are dumb too.

*Finch Eggs*

106

# June Bird Report
# For a Topanga Neighborhood.

Ken Wheeland and I live across the street from each other so we are able to support each other in covering the bird life of our properties in a fairly intensive manner. We've been particularly active in covering avian activities in the month of June. This is probably the busiest time in the life of most birds— the time for mating, laying eggs, incubating, feeding young and teaching them to live independently.

This year has been particularly exciting for us. Our first bonanza was to have a pair of Red-tailed Hawks nest within easy binocular viewing so we could watch daily progress. A pair (perhaps the same ones) nested in the hills above us last year but we only discovered them when the noisy fledglings left home and went cruising around, chasing after their parents to get fed.

Another first was a Phainopepla nesting family. This species is fairly common nesting in our uphill meadows, but this was their first foray into our neighborhood. This is the one bird I know that habitually carries on its family functioning in a ménage a trois. Two males share with one female the chores of building a nest, incubating the eggs and raising the young. They also have the distinction of habitually raising two broods a year in two very different places. In January they nest in the deserts of Arizona and California and in the spring they come up to the mountains to do it all over again. This relatively stressful schedule may be why the female requires two males in attendance.

Dark-eyed Juncos have been abundant winter birds throughout the Santa Monica Mountains but a rare breeding bird in Topanga. An exception when I arrived forty years ago was a pair which was nesting every year in a flower pot at Camp Wildwood. Breeding in our neighborhood was certified for this year when Ken found two fledglings in his vestibule. Since then, the nesting among Juncos has been increasing until now they are a regular among the breeders in Topanga.

Two other first-time nesters on our property have been Acorn Woodpeckers and Band-tailed Pigeons. There has been a colony of the woodpeckers across the road from the Inn of the Seventh Ray for many years. They have preempted a utility pole on Old Canyon Road on which they maintain their tradition of keeping a collective supply of acorns for the whole colony. The species has been expanding and there is another group at Trippet Ranch as well as the beginnings of one in our neighborhood. The introduction of the Band-tails is also a part of an increase of the species in California.

Other species we have nesting on or near our property include the following: Song Sparrow, California Towhee, Spotted Towhee, Oak Titmouse, Hooded Oriole, Bullock's Oriole, Black-headed Grosbeak, Lesser Goldfinch, Robin, Starling, Crow, Mourning Dove, Nuttall's Woodpecker, Downy Woodpecker, Flicker, Black Phoebe, Pacific-slope Flycatcher, House Wren, Bushtit, Wrentit, House Finch, Anna's Hummingbird, Allen's Hummingbird, Mockingbird, Hutton's Vireo, and Orange-crowned Warbler.

**Part 3:**

# More Thoughts on the Cowbird

# Doing the Darwinian Dance:
# In the Trenches with a Cowbird's Struggle for Survival

I am fascinated by Cowbirds. It is the one bird we know in the western hemisphere which does not raise its own young. It lays its eggs in other birds' nests to be hatched and raised by the other species which is always, by choice, smaller than the Cowbird. (There is a bird in Europe which exhibits this same strange behavior. It is called the Cuckoo. I wonder why?)

The habit of dumping its eggs on other birds to care for is a serious departure from the human moral code and has created some strong feelings among bird lovers. For example, John Burroughs, an outstanding naturalist at the turn of the century, described the maternal and domestic character of the cowbird as "thoroughly bad .... An unnatural mother in breeding season may be seen skulking about ...seeking for nests in which to place a surreptitious egg... selecting in a cowardly way a small nest leaving the care of its young to the tender mercies of some already burdened little mother... In keeping with its unclean habits and unholy life and character, the cowbird's ordinary note is a gurgling, rasping whistle."

John Burroughs makes a very strong judgmental case against the cowbird. It sounds like he has really gone overboard. But I recently ran across the following written by me when I was a teenager and had just learned about the bird's lifestyle but had not yet read the judgmental reactions of others.

At that time, [1938] I wrote: "What right do they have to lay their bigger egg in a smaller bird's nest and leave it there to hatch sooner and grow faster until the bully pushes out most or all the rightful owners' young, leaving only a fat ugly Cowbird demanding to be raised to maturity by a sleek lovely pair of warblers or the like? We should start a campaign to seek out and find cowbird eggs and smash them." My outburst was triggered by finding two adult Blue-gray Gnatcatchers (a bird about the size of a wren) frenetically dashing about to satisfy the food needs of an immature cowbird which looked almost as big as the two of them together. Of course, there was no sign of any young Gnatcatchers about. Their lives had probably been sacrificed for the survival of the Cowbird.

My attitude toward Cowbirds has mellowed over the years. Two factors contributed to this change. One was the experience of a friend who had just returned from living abroad for a number of years. He told me he was considerably upset by having left an un-born child in the belly of a woman who was about to marry another man with the intention that the two of them would raise the child together. A stranger was to replace him as the father of his child. While he was telling me his troubled tale, a Cowbird came to my feeder. I pointed to the bird and told my friend how the Cowbird gets other birds to raise its young. He went away, feeling less alone in the universe.

The other factor which helped me gain a different perspective about the cowbird was learning how they may have come to live the way they do. When Europeans first came to America, they found no Cowbirds here. When Lewis and Clark went on their voyage of discovery, one of their most spectacular discoveries was the buffalo herds which migrated by the millions up and down the Great Plains. Accompanying the buffalo were flocks of birds which ran in and out among their feet, feeding on the billions of insects which were stirred up by the hooves. Lewis and Clark gave them the name of Buffalo Birds.

Given the continuous movement of the herds, the Buffalo Birds during breeding season would be faced with the choice between raising their own young or staying with the herd. Apparently staying with the Buffalo won out. (I wonder if the choice was unanimous? Was it immediate or did it take a period of years for all of the birds to behave uniformly as they do now?)

The new breeding pattern must have worked out okay for a time but eventually the Buffalo were exterminated as the plains were converted into agricultural land. As the land was gradually transformed into farms and ranches, cows replaced the buffalo and the birds involved with the herds switched their dependency to the new host, requiring the name change from "Buffalo Bird" to "Cowbird".

We may wonder why the Cowbirds didn't take advantage of their new host staying put, which would enable them to raise their young the way birds 'are supposed to,' but as long as their unique system worked, maybe they just enjoy their unique brand of parental freedom.

I got so immersed in thinking about Cowbirds that I began dreaming about them. My dreams became so real that it began to seem as though I had really been a Cowbird. One thing which may have made it easy was that I already had a history of imagining I was a cowboy. Maybe I was a cowboy or a Cowbird in a previous life. If that seems crazy to you, remember there are millions of people in the world who believe in reincarnation. Anyhow, here is my story:

# My Life as a Cowbird

Once I was a lonely Cowbird.
Someone must have dumped me
in a nest of strangers.
I feel like I don't belong here.
Four weirdoes share this nest with me.
I don't understand a word they say
nor do they understand me.

We have two grown up birds
whose full time job seems to be feeding us.
That keeps them busy all the time.
They try to feed us in turn
but I'm bigger than the rest
and I need more food.
So I figured out a way to get more food.

When a feeder comes with food
it  perches just above the chick
whose turn it is to be fed.
I maneuver myself alongside that chick.
When the feeder starts bending over
I quickly bump the chick aside
and stick my great big mouth
right where its little mouth had been.
So you can bet that I kept getting bigger
while some of the others
seemed to stop growing.

continues

The next big problem we had was
it began getting crowded in the nest.
I finally figured out how to fix that problem.
While the feeders were away,
I snuggled up to one of the chicks,
managed to work my way under it
and I gave it the old "heave-ho,
right up, and out, and away you go."
The other chicks started howling.
They didn't seem to appreciate
that we were all more comfortable
by being less crowded.
I just ignored their lack of gratitude.
When the feeders came back
they didn't seem to notice
anyone was missing.
I guess all they saw
was a mess of open mouths
wailing and waiting for food.

Time went on and we started getting crowded again.
Time for another chick to go.
Time to give the old "heave-ho".
This time the remaining chicks kept their mouths shut, probably
wondering if they would be next.
And, sure enough, they were.

The main problem was no longer limited space,
but the limited amount of food.
I finally needed all the morsels
the two feeders could come up with.
So I had to bump out the last of the competition.
Funny thing, after I did this,
I started getting lonely,
almost as if I missed those dumb chicks!

So I set off to explore the world.
Only I was afraid the feeders
might not find me
if I wasn't in the nest.
So at first I didn't go far from the nest.
When I was out exploring
I kept an eye out for the feeders.
When I saw one of them nearby
I would howl as loud as I could
and discovered that they were just as loyal to me
as they had been to their own family.
When they heard me howl they came right to me.

continues

I was perched near the end of a branch
one time when a bug smacked into my face.
Quick as a wink I turned,
caught it in my beak
and swallowed it.
It tasted delicious!
It was a lot better
than the second-hand stuff
the feeders had been stuffing me with.

That was the beginning of my independence.
I quickly learned to feed myself full time
and let my feeders get lost.

*Cowbird*

# The Lone Adolescent.

A week or two after the Cowbird went out on his own, I was riding a horse within a mile of the nesting site where the Darwinian Drama had been taking place. As I was riding through a meadow, a drab gray-brown bird flew up in front of my horse's hooves and went walking a little distance away. I noted the walking behavior and the fact that it kept its tail elevated behind it, both of which characterized it as a Cowbird. I decided that it might very likely be the very Cowbird whose life I have been describing thus far.

It was the only immature bird I saw alone at this time of year. All the other young were still in small family groups, including two parents who were helping the youngsters to learn about the world. The realization struck me strongly that the Cowbird is unique in beginning its life as a loner.

Does it feel lonely? Is it looking for other birds that are similar to itself? How will it recognize other Cowbirds when it has no idea how it looks itself? Maybe by voice alone. Has anybody ever studied two Cowbirds discovering each other for the first time?

Perhaps my adolescent Cowbird doesn't feel at all lonely

because it doesn't know yet that it is missing anything. Perhaps it will come as a delightful surprise to discover that there is "someone just like me" in the universe. How would it be for us humans to discover that there are beings just like us out there in the Universe? Of course, the surprise for us has been muted by all the fantasies our cartoonists have deluged our comics and our movie screens with about creatures from outer space.

Does the Cowbird ever learn to be social? If so, how social? Would you believe that this Cowbird will probably become a member of one of the largest flocks of birds in the world? It is one of the blackbirds and as such may join a group a million strong in Louisiana and Mississippi.

**Part 4:**

# Raptors

# Raptor Rapture

Two sleek White-tailed Kites,
perched in a small tree
which stands alone in a meadow,
are soaking up the light and heat
of the morning sun.
Their breasts are bright white
against the dark of a distant hill.
She whistles plaintively.
He raises his wings
and slips gracefully over to her.
In a sedate and dignified ritual,
two wings raised, two wings drooped,
they copulate for a moment,
making their commitment to the next generation.

Near the hill a Harrier courses
back and forth over the meadow
scouting the grasses below
for a rodent repast
to appease his aching hunger.

An oak woodland borders one edge of the meadow.
Four acres of the sky above that woods
are churning with the raucous sound
and turbulent motion
of two hawks, Red-shouldered,
diving and swooping up,
swerving and twisting,
bolting and chasing,
screaming all the while.
Carrying on a wild courtship,
they fight to a climax
which also, however belligerently,
makes a commitment to the next generation.

# Lord of the Night

The stillness of a winter night is broken a few hours before dawn by a deep, bass 'boooom -boooom — boom-boom — boooom'. The sound carries a very long distance across the valley and up the canyons. An anxious, insomniac Californian, worrying about The Big One, hears it and imagines it to be the rumbling of the earth. A love-lorn wanderer longing for the lady he left behind thinks he hears the mournful moaning of a distant train.

Wild creatures, foraging or roosting in the dark, hear the voice of death. For them the sound stirs up the same terror as the midnight roar of a lion on the Serengeti plains. Appropriately so, because this sound proclaims the presence of the Lord of the Night, the Great Horned Owl.

Pound for pound, the Great Horned Owl is one of the most ferocious predators in the world. It takes down geese and turkeys many times its own weight. It kills and devours the skunk, despite the latter's aromatic, defense. It preys upon the porcupine despite the poisonous quills. Nor does it spare other predators, feasting at times on hawks and other owls. One was even observed driving off a Bald Eagle to take possession of the nesting site of that majestic symbol of America's martial pride.

Knowing the fierce reputation of this bird, I was feeling quite nervous while approaching a nest filled with young in Topanga. Hearing them hooting at night or seeing one perched on a utility pole in the daytime is one thing. Transgressing on their home ground is quite another, particularly when one knows that the literature abounds in reports of men suffering severe wounds from attacks by the owl near its nest.

As I walked carefully on a narrow shelf across the face of a cliff toward the nesting cave, I stopped repeatedly to look around for the parents. As I got near the fully grown but downy owlets, I took my camera in both hands and sighted through the viewfinder, well aware of my vulnerability to the rear in this position. I moved close enough to the young to fill the frame with their bodies and began to shoot. As I began snapping my shutter, the owlets assumed a ferocious expression and began snapping back with their beaks. I felt reasonably safe until I heard the snapping of a beak behind me. I tingled with fear, knowing that a parent was on guard and was giving me warning signals. I shot two more quick photos and rapidly left the scene.

# The Great Owl is a Great Survivor

Owls are marvelously adapted to hunting in the still of the night. One of their skills is to be able to fly in absolute silence. They are able to do this because the leading edge of their wings is serrated, disrupting the flow of air and thus eliminating noise caused by airflow over a smooth surface.

Another hunting skill of owls is their ability to locate prey precisely in absolute darkness. The difference in time when sound reaches each ear is used by them to tell where the source is on the horizontal plane. For example, if the sound reaches both ears at the same time, then the source is directly ahead.

Location on the vertical plane is made possible by the fact that the opening on one ear is high and the opening on the other is low. Variations in intensity of sound perceived in each ear indicate to owls how high or low the source is. Thus, a sound equally loud must be at eye level.

Owls' ears are linked to specific parts of the brain in such a way that they carry in their head a detailed map of their immediate environment with auditory coordinates.

This extraordinary set of adaptations must have taken an exceedingly long time to evolve. By human standards, the Great Horned Owl has been on this planet an exceedingly long time. It is elite among all living owls in being related to the oldest owl fossils thus far discovered. These have been dated to sixty million years ago. We humans are relatively new kids on the sphere, going back less than four million years. Will our own species survive as long a time on this planet Earth? One part of this question is the broader question of whether culturally determined adaptations will prove to have as much survival value as genetically determined adaptations. Who is more fit to survive, Homo Sapiens or the Great Horned Owl?

Shifting away from a competitive context, consider the wonder that there has evolved on spaceship Earth this marvelous owl with its exquisite capacity to penetrate absolute darkness in precisely locating objects in space! Then consider that on this same planet has evolved another creature which has penetrated the darkness to discover the intricate mechanisms by which the owl performs its feat!

We humans carry consciousness and appreciation for the universe, thereby rounding out the cycle of cosmic creativity.

# Lord of the Night Revisited

The first bird song of every day in Topanga (as differentiated from a bird which sings all night long like the Mockingbird) is the "hoo—hoo—hu-hoot" of the Great Horned Owl. Any of us anywhere in Topanga who are lucky enough to be awake at 4 A. M. have a very good chance of hearing this call.

Every year during Christmas week a few hardy birders meet at the Post Office at 4 and spread out over our community to listen for owls. We usually hear one or two Screech Owls, a few Barn Owls and always between twenty-five and thirty Great Horned Owls. (This is a part of our contribution to the annual Audubon bird census.) Our count may indicate that the Great Horned is our most common owl or it may be a function of the fact that this bird does not have to be afraid to announce his presence because he is the most powerful avian predator anywhere around. Any other owl calling runs the risk of becoming prey.

Topanga Horned Owls start nesting in February. Since it takes four months before eggs convert to owls that can fly, many of their nests in April still contain very large and ravenously hungry young. I wrote the following poem to recount my experience with one such nest:

# Hoot-Owl Puppies

Hoot-owl Puppies, standing at attention,
just as still as if stuffed,
carrying an air of solemn dignity
despite their fluffy down coats.
They look down on me
from the entrance to their cave
high in a redrock cliff.
I climb a hill and walk a path.
They follow my every movement,
but only with their eyeballs.
Did they have the same teacher
as the guards at Buckingham Palace?

Never having used their wings,
when they watch me walking,
do they feel a biped kinship with me?

Or do they firmly believe that one day
they will master the miracle of flight
like the parents who fly to them regularly
with rodents and rattlers?

# End of the Hunt

Our Lady of the Hummingbirds was surveying her flock, making sure that all twenty-four portals were well supplied, when she heard a thrashing sound coming down from the hillside which bordered her backyard. She was expecting to see a Mule Deer or two but instead, when she looked up, she saw two large birds rise up from the ground and come toward her. They were soaring, stiff-winged, directly at her and she prepared to duck but they passed overhead. The one in the lead was badly battered—its feathers ruffled badly, even a few missing. It was uttering a pitiful cry, almost like a baby.

The pursuer was a large Red-tailed Hawk sounding off with a loud, proud victory call. The two birds went by and disappeared around a corner of the house. Donna followed only to the corner and, not wanting to stop the Red-tail at his feeding ceremony, merely took a peek. She saw the Red-tail astride his prey, his wings raised in the characteristic mantling posture of a successful raptor.

Having witnessed the mantling, Donna ducked back out of sight and did not return to the site until the next morning. All that remained was two piles of feathers which posed a mystery:

1. Had the hawk consumed the entire feast and left two plies of feathers neatly behind?

2. Had he consumed half the feast (accounting for one pile of feathers) then plucked the other half (accounting for the second pile), returning the meat to his mate?

3. Or what do you think?

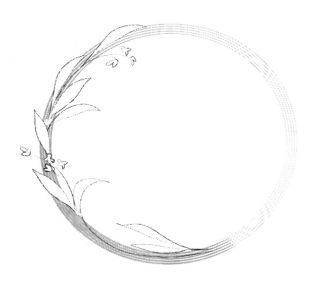

# Coyotes Attack Pyrocantha

Contrary to what some of you may be thinking, Pyrocantha is not some kind of Python. It is not even a snake. It is a bush which sports bright red berries when it is in fruit. These are a special delicacy for and are consumed in quantity by a number of bird species. Cedar Waxwings and Robins are particularly fond of them. During the winter both birds gather in large flocks at the same time that the Pyrocantha berries ripen. A flock of forty or fifty Waxwings may settle in a large patch of the berries and clean them out in three or four days. One time I saw a flock of about a thousand Robins clean out a very large patch of berries in one full day.

Birds, yes, but large mammals? Hardly. The berries are high enough that they would necessitate an animal without wings to climb up the bush to get at them. The bush is delicate enough that a small squirrel is about as much weight as the branches can bear.

So one day when Donna, Our Lady of the Hummingbirds, saw a coyote in her backyard gazing up at her Pyrocantha bush, she felt compassion for him. She knew he would like to forage on those red berries, but she could see that they were well beyond his reach.

Suddenly, to her surprise, he leaped into the air farther than she had ever dreamed a coyote could jump. At the top of his leap he grabbed a mouthful of berries and, descending to earth, proceeded to gulp them down.

The coyote continued leaping and gulping for the rest of that day and returned the next day to continue the job until all the berries were gone.

Another coyote foraging enterprise was observed by Donna in her backyard. Her premises were regularly patrolled by a pair which was identifiable by the fact that one of them had no tail. She inferred that No Tail was the male because, whenever they appeared together he was in the lead. (The male pronoun used in the Pyrocantha segment of this story indicates that No Tail was the central character therein.)

Donna had a table in her yard which she used for feeding birds. It was above the line of sight for the coyotes but one day she put a crust of bread out just before dusk. No Tail arrived in time to see her put the food out...waited until she went indoors ...ran over... jumped up and snatched the bread and left.

The next day Mrs. Coyote came early to the yard and jumped up on the table, something she had never done before. The only way Donna could explain this behavior was that No Tail must have communicated to his mate about checking on the table for food.

If it seems strange that coyotes can communicate such information to each other, consider the fact that bees are known to do so. A lone bee can return to the hive from a long distance away and let his fellows know that he has found a large patch of flowers blooming there. He does this by doing a dance inside the hive. The bees are able to leave the informer behind and fly directly to the patch with the information which they received from the dance.

# Poetry, Power and the Peregrine:
# Falcon of the Gods

The capacity of the Peregrine to stir the human soul was born out for me on a recent visit to the Malibu Lagoon. I was leisurely enjoying a peaceful island vista from the nearby shore. A thousand gulls standing serenely on a sandbar, all facing in the same direction, gave the appearance of a snowfield in repose. There were only small flurries of movement, as if a soft breeze were sporadically kicking up a few flakes here and there across the mass.

Suddenly the scene exploded. The sand bar was transformed from white to brown and the air filled with wildly beating wings as all the gulls tore off for the open ocean. All this frantic flight was in response to the sudden appearance of a Peregrine which circled the retreating flock and then flew along beside it. It made a few unsuccessful passes at individual gulls and then, as they were flying over the beach, it maneuvered one down toward the sand, but as the Peregrine lunged, the gull twisted away and also escaped.

As the birds disappeared over the ocean, I found my heart beating wildly. I was completely captivated by the dramatic power of the Peregrine to instigate such a fleeing frenzy in a mass of birds, each of which was bigger than itself. I immediately understood why the Kings of Europe, the Shoguns of Japan, and the Sheiks of Arabia were willing to pay small fortunes to possess one of these birds.

How did the gulls all sense the danger so quickly and simultaneously? Prey birds seem to recognize the shape of predators by instinct. Konrad Lorenz has shown that newborn chicks can differentiate between two images of a plywood silhouette pulled across the barnyard. When it is pulled in one direction, it looks like a falcon and the chicks run for cover. When it is pulled in the other direction, it looks like a goose and the chicks continue feeding.

The peregrine flew to the end of the flock then turned and flew alongside it. He made a few feints at individual gulls and then, just as he reached the beach, he swooped down at one which was close to the sand. He missed on all three of these attempts, which was not surprising since the gulls were all highly aware of his presence. I lost him as all the birds moved out to sea.

A few minutes later, however, the Peregrine came back, flying over the lagoon in the opposite direction from before. At the upper end, he began to soar in circles, rising higher and higher. He got smaller and smaller in my binoculars and then momentarily, I couldn't see him with my naked eye. Nor could I find him again in the glass when I tried. I kept staring into the area where he had disappeared. After a bit, I thought I saw a spot moving downward. It got larger and larger until it took the form of a bird. It was the falcon diving very, very fast! At the bottom of his dive, he crashed into a duck which was flying over the lagoon. I had an instant fear that the collision might be fatal to both. The duck was tumbling inertly down, almost like a wooden decoy. But the falcon was still very much alive. He flew under the duck, turned upside down and grabbed it with his talons. Then he turned right side up again and flew off with his prey to disappear among some willows on the far side of the lagoon.

I shouted out loud, exhilarated by the sheer explosive power of the scene. I felt captivated by the majestic falcon. I felt him to be an extension of myself: it was I who had terrified thousands of gulls, sending them fleeing out to sea; it was I who had soared to a height beyond the power of humans to see and from that height, I had spotted a mallard and took aim. I had dived in pursuit at express train speed. I had stunned my prey with my hurtling body then plucked the duck right out of the air.

We almost lost the Peregrine Falcon here in the USA. We almost lost that magnificent bird to high-tech agriculture. With ever increasing efficiency in producing fodder for our bellies, we almost drove to extinction a legendary source of food for our souls.

Our Peregrines were almost wiped out by DDT, widely used in agriculture. The Peregrine feeds almost exclusively on other birds, which places it at the top of the food chain. Being on top may be prestigious in our celebrity conscious culture but it can also be dangerous. Most birds ingesting DDT were not adversely affected: this toxic chemical is found in harmless amounts in prey birds low on the food chain but accumulates in predators at the top in amounts large enough to interfere with female production of calcium. Consequently, eggshells became so thin as to break under the weight of the incubating bird, thus making it impossible for the falcons to reproduce. During the 1960s, Peregrines disappeared entirely from east of the Mississippi and, in California, were reduced to just a few breeding pairs.

By the early '70s, it was clearly documented that the Peregrine was rapidly disappearing as a result of the use of DDT. Fortunately, we humans are sometimes able to heal the wounds we inflict upon the world. The federal government stepped in to ban the use of DDT on our farmlands, thus eliminating the source of the problem. However, the population of Peregrines had been reduced so drastically that it was questionable whether they would be able to come back on their own.

Cornell University ornithologist Tom Cade responded to this problem by developing a two-phase falcon farm. He borrowed three pairs of Peregrines from falconers and raised the young they produced. He also collected eggs in the wild as soon as they were laid and took them back to his laboratory to be incubated. Usually, when a nesting is disturbed, parents will later on lay another clutch of eggs. By the time they did, Cade's first clutch had hatched and he exchanged the newly hatched young for the second clutch of eggs. These young were left for the wild birds to raise while Cade and his cohorts incubated and raised the second setting in the laboratory. This program worked so well that it attracted volunteer support to fund it and it was extended to Fort Collins, Colorado and Santa Cruz, California.

Some of the birds raised in Santa Cruz were released from the roof of the Glendon-Tivertan building two blocks from my office in Westwood. This release site was chosen after a number of young falcons released from Boney Ridge near Sycamore Canyon were lost to Great Homed Owls before they adapted fully to the wild. It was exciting for me to spend my lunch hour watching the young Peregrines play high-speed tag with each other in the air space around their high-rise home.

Twenty years after Cade created the Peregrine breeding project, the bird is reestablished throughout its former range.

This world of ours is deeply enriched by the presence of a bird which can stir up such strong emotions. What a tragedy if they had slipped away from us into extinction.

It is a great triumph for us to be able to say now that the Peregrines are back in the USA!

# Terrorist Attack on a Covey of Quail

I stepped out on my back lawn at that time of day when most of the world is at rest. It was hot. It was still. It was very, very quiet.

Two Brown Towhees were desultorily pecking at seeds under our bird feeder. They are part of a small family which has adopted our yard as their home. They are also part of the largest bird family in our Santa Monica Mountains. They flew into a nearby tree as I went by. It is always comforting to see them happily at home with us, even when I only see them on my way to elsewhere. I walked down to our box canyon with its redwood deck and small pool of rocks and concrete, I sat in a chair on the deck to meditate in this most spiritually nourishing spot on our property.

Sometime later, I became aware of crackling leaves in the thick underbrush. Beside me I peered into the shadows and saw an indeterminate number of small, plump dark shapes which I first saw as mammals and then finally as birds of some sort scratching on the ground. As the Birdman of Topanga, I feel it is my duty to know the names of all the birds I see here, and these were not immediately identifiable. I was relieved when a larger bird flew away from the flock to a branch three feet above ground and was revealed as a male California Quail. He was beautifully plumaged in soft blues, whites, blacks, and grays. I identified him as the proud father of the family.

As if posing for a photo op, the leader of the clan sang forth a rousing "Chip, chip, chip—Chicago," which is the way the song is described in bird guides written by easterners. Since this is the signature song of the California Quail, it seems to me much more appropriate to hear it as "Chip, chip, chip—Amigo."

Despite the difference among birders interpreting the call, the birds themselves reacted to it as a rallying cry. The young immediately began emerging from the shadows until Voila! There were nine milling around their parent.

I just had time to count the family when suddenly the mass exploded with a loud roar, fragments flying in every direction and almost immediately every individual was hidden in the surrounding brush! I was not only startled, but very puzzled until a Cooper's Hawk flew over the now vacated assembly grounds, and I understood the impetus for the exodus I had witnessed. The Cooper's Hawk is an Acciptiter and they are the deadliest killers of birds in the Santa Monica Mountains. Other hawks have to find their prey in the open but the Accipiter is so designed that he can pursue his prey through the trees.

I was deeply impressed by the rapidity and coordination of the response to danger. Who had seen the hawk coming and how was that message communicated to the mass? The father of the family must have been the one to see the Accipiter, because he was the only one on watch. He was undoubtedly genetically imprinted to identify the shape as ENEMY!

Because even newborn chicks have been discovered to flee when they see a hawk in flight, his immediate projection of his body into the air was followed so closely by his offspring that they all seemed to explode simultaneously.

Earlier in the week I had been watching repeated TV showings of the terrorist attack upon the N.Y. Towers so it was inevitable that I made some comparisons between the two events:

1. Without advance warning, the threat comes out
   of the air.
2. The threat is delivered by an instrument with wings.
3. The threat targets a relatively densely packed group.
4. The target group is engaged in everyday peaceful activity.
5. Most of the threatened individuals had no warning
   and probably never even saw the threat.

The major difference between the two events was that there were no victims in the box canyon. All of the Quail survived. The Hawk aborted his attack and kept on flying down the canyon and out of sight.

After the Accipiter left, the young began emerging from the brush again, nervously milling about until they heard their signature song ring out again: "Chip, Chip, Chip, Amigo." It came from the brush across the pond. Father was rallying his family to follow him on a hidden trail up the face of a cliff bordering that side of the pond. A single file began to form; the young ones following each other by sight and sound—they were uttering their soft twang as they went—and stopping whenever a seed or berry caught their attention. The path crisscrossed the cliff a number of times until it reached the top and the group passed over and out of sight and probably out of danger.

The contrast between the two incidents left me thinking pensively; if only there had been a father watching over us in New York City!

*Covey of Quail*

# The Kestrel and the Shrike

An elegant bird is poised on the topmost branch of a young oak. It presents a princely image with its coat of slaty blue and russet adorned with striking patterns of black, white and beige in stripes and splotches. Its heavy beak and large talons identify it as a bird of prey. Its pointed wings, long tail and tear-drop marks under the eye denote it as a falcon. It is a Kestrel, the smallest North American falcon.

The Kestrel has just been chasing a Flicker, probably just for sport, since the woodpecker is somewhat larger than the falcon and would be difficult to handle. Now it has gotten serious and has taken a post from which it is scanning the broad meadow spreading out from the base of the oak.

Another bird flies into the tree and perches at the top of a branch within ten feet of the falcon. This bird, with its black mask across the eyes and hooked beak, looks like a bandit. Its body is white, its wings and back are gray. It is a Shrike. Although it looks much like a raptor, it is actually a songbird.

While the Kestrel seems completely indifferent to its new neighbor, the Shrike is agitatedly aware of the Kestrel. It glances over repeatedly and from time to time drops into the lower leafy branches and approaches the falcon, calling raucously. Before covering half the distance across, it turns and creeps silently back to its lookout perch. Why is this songbird so interested in the hawk?

After a long period of waiting, a small flock of sparrows flies into a nearby portion of the meadow and settles down to feed on seeds. Immediately the Kestrel dives and disappears momentarily in the weeds. A feathered explosion erupts around him as finches flee for cover. The Kestrel rises from the ground clutching a bird in its talons and flies off with it.

The Shrike launches his attack a moment later, dashing madly into the oaks after the sparrows. Without the advantage of surprise, the odds are against the pursuer in dense foliage and the sparrows successfully elude him. He soon gives up and flies to another lookout perch on the north end of the meadow.

The Kestrel and the Shrike are in many ways similar although they come from two very different evolutionary strains. Both of them are loners which forage over meadows and prey upon large insects, small birds and rodents. Each frequently hovers while hunting. They both have "teeth" on their upper bill and corresponding notches on the lower bill, a highly specific structure which has only evolved in shrikes and falcons and which is very useful in tearing apart prey. Finally, the names of these two birds have similar derivations. "Shrike" comes from an old English word meaning "shriek" and "Kestrel" comes from a Latin word meaning "rattle, creak or crackle".

Despite all their similarities, the Kestrel and the Shrike have very different evolutionary histories. The Kestrel is a Raptor, a family which has evolved over millions of years to specialize in catching prey. The Shrike is a Songbird, a family which has also evolved over millions of years but NOT specializing in capturing prey. Indeed, the Shrike might be considered the black sheep of the family, cannibalizing fellow family members.

The major disadvantage of the Shrike's sonqbird status is its small songbird feet. This has led to the bird having a bad reputation. Without talons, it is unable to hold prey firmly either for transporting or for holding while it tears it into edible portions. It has therefore had to improvise, which it frequently does by impaling the captured bird on barbed wire. This practice has earned it the name "butcher bird" and a considerable attendant amount of disapproval.

Shrikes are probably still evolving as predators. Some of this development may be through learning. The Shrike which was so interested in the Kestrel may well have been trying to pick up some of the tricks of the predatory trade from a master.

YIKES! Shrikes Return!

The Shrike has returned to his winter home in Raptor Meadow, Topanga. He has reclaimed his favorite perch at the top of a large elderberry bush in the center of the meadow. He surveys the surrounding territory from the highest point in a sea of brown grasses-rye, curly dock, foxtail etc. Perched prominently as he is, the Shrike strikes a commanding presence. In contrast with his gray and white body, he wears a black mask across his eyes which, with his hooked beak, makes him look as sinister as a pirate.

The Shrike's piratical appearance contributes to his evil reputation which, however, is largely based on his habit of impaling songbirds on barbed wire so he can rip off their flesh with his large bill.

Although others may shudder in horrified disapproval, I forgive the Shrike his barbaric eating habits. Having somehow developed a taste for songbirds, he is confronted by a structural limitation in that his feet are designed for perching and not for holding prey. His adaptation to that shortcoming is to substitute barbed wire and thorns for the talons that raptors possess.

As I reread my apology for the Shrike's vicious behavior, I wonder if some of you may think that I have a vicious streak of my own. By way of deflating a possible righteous stance among my readers, I would like to pose the question: "Which do you admire more, a sparrow or a hawk?" Then consider how each prepares his food for swallowing.

As I watch a sparrow writhing on barbed wire where it is has been impaled by a shrike, I feel a corresponding writhing going on in my own stomach. Am I feeling pangs of sympathy for the victim or exulting in the cruelty of the predator?

I dreamed once that I was an old gobbler locked in a cage and that my belly was being ripped apart by three young gobblers. I remember accepting my fate and admiring the young Turks for their rapacious assault. Weird perhaps, but Jungian analysts inform us that our collective unconscious contains archetypes for both the sacrificial lamb and for Bluebeard.

Responding to our inner lamb, our impulse might be to empathize with the weak and the helpless plight of the victim. Responding to our inner Bluebeard, we might have the opposite impulse, to relish the ravaging of the victim. My dream seems to reflect identification with both archetypes.

It seems easy for me to feel good about myself over feeling sorry for the victim, but I have to justify my identification with the aggressor. I find support for that part of me in Thoreau's confession of his savage desire to seize a woodchuck and devour it on the spot, ripping out its bloody flesh and its life with his own hands and teeth.

What is your attitude toward the Shrike? To what extent do

you abhor? To what extent do you admire? If you knew you were going to be a bird in your next life and you had to choose, would you be a Shrike or a sparrow?

*Kestral*

# A Plague of Hawks

Since the middle of March, irritating noises have been grating on the nerves of a number of Topangans. The offending decibels apparently emanate from the woodland surrounding our houses. Fred Feer describes the offenders as a plague of hawks. He has seen three hawk-like birds perched in trees on his grounds uttering loud, high-pitched screeches every so often all day long. At least a half dozen others have reported a similar phenomenon.

Since summer arrived on Solstice Day, my wife Lynne and my neighbor Ken have reported similar screeching but at a somewhat lower pitch and during the night.

I was able to hear the daytime screeching when Lynne pointed it out to me, but I have to take their word for the nighttime serenade. I happen to be blessed with poor hearing, and when I take out my hearing aids at night, silence reigns supreme. I can't even hear the traffic on the boulevard which sometimes keeps Lynne from dozing off. It took a whole cavalcade of motorcycles one Sunday night to keep me awake while I roundly cursed the Harley boys and imagined them as adult replicas of the burly bully in high school who got his kicks out of emitting loud farts during particularly peaceful sessions in the classroom.

With all this screeching going on day and night, it was inevitable that someone would ask "the Birdman of Topanga" what it was all about. The answer I came up with is that we have here a case of an adolescent appetite coupled with infantile skills in foraging and a large measure of childlike impatience. The noise is being made by young raptors, hawks by day, owls by night, which are fully as large as their parents but have yet to learn how to hunt and get their own food. Their screeching is their way of trying to get their parents to feed them pronto. However, it often takes their parents a long time to find food. John Burroughs reports one experience of a Red-tailed Hawk soaring from 7:00 in the morning until 4:00 in the afternoon before he swooped down to make a kill. Young birds clearly don't understand why it takes so long, and it will take them six or more weeks after fledging before they are able to hunt for themselves. Until they mature to that point, we harassed humans have to put up with their loud complaining.

# Cooper's Hawk and the Hush of Death

The assassin burst from the dark woods and cut along the interface between grove and field, screaming all the way.

She perched in a dead tree on a distant hill, obviously wanting to draw me toward her.

However, I already knew that her nest with three young was just inside the grove from which she had emerged, so I was not fooled into following her.

The assassin here is a Cooper's Hawk, a raptor that by virtue of its accomplishments is known as the deadliest killer of songbirds in the U.S.

When its loud "cucks" ring through the woods of June, the hush of death pervades everything. All small birds become still and silent.

The presence of a Cooper's Hawk always brings a chill to the heart of the poultry farmer. Its predations upon pullets are so extensive that it is called "chicken hawk"—a label that is often extended indiscriminately and undeservedly to many other raptors.

Before going into the trees to observe the nest, I "glassed" the hawk and saw that she was being pestered by a small bird which was fluttering around her head, and repeatedly diving down to peck her scalp. The distance was too great for me to identify the little one.

After watching the big bird/little bird drama for a while, I went on toward the hawks nest.

Almost immediately I heard a rising crescendo of approaching screeches, and turned to see the female bulleting right at me. She seemed intent on doing unto me that which had been done unto her by the little bird.

At the last moment she veered slightly away, and passed over to alight on a nearby branch on my other side.

Suddenly I saw that the little bird was back on the job-fluttering above and dive-bombing the hawk's head, and was soon joined by another of its kind. They were close enough now for me to see that they were Gnatcatchers.

I was admiring their feisty behavior in bedeviling the hawk when I understood, in one of those moments, their similarity to the Mockingbird which has the same aggressive habits in driving off large pests like hawks, crows and cats.

Both of these species are predominantly gray and white so that the Gnatcatcher looks very much like a small, trim Mockingbird.

"The most expressive feature of the Gnatcatcher and of its larger counterpart, the Mockingbirds is its long, ever active tail; now up and down, now from side to side, it is never for an instant at rest. Under stress, (as in its present role of tormenting a dangerous hawk) the bird seems to combine the two motions at once and achieves a ludicrous impression of circular motion." (Bent, 1949)

The Cooper paid no attention to her tormenters, and made two more feints at me before I finally left.

Although I admired both aggressors for their daring behavior, I don't think that either the female hawk or I sensed any real personal danger in the attacks being made upon us.

On my way home I saw the male Cooper's Hawk far off to the side of the grove.

I remembered when I first arrived an hour before that I had seen him as a shadowy figure somewhere in the vicinity of the nest, flying silently away toward the edge where he was now perched. He apparently had no investment in defending his home at least not in the vigorously confrontational manner of his mate.

I felt a little ashamed for him. I wondered later why the Gnatcatchers were so persistent that day in their attacks upon this particular Cooper's Hawk. Returning, I eventually found their nest not 200 yards from the hawk's nest. On following visits I learned that these plucky little ones had successfully fledged five offspring, while the assassins raised three young.

*Cooper's Hawk*

# Hawks, Gophers, and Broken Wings

We have had a young hawk displaying some odd behavior on the roof of our little office building behind our house. The young one has just been learning to fly, having fledged in a nest high in a pine tree alongside Gilbey Trail; which is the name denoting our driveway on old maps of Topanga. The Gilbey bird is as large as his red-tailed parents but has been flying away from his nest for only a week.

Around a week after leaving the nest for the first time, we noticed the bird lying prone on its belly. It stayed flattened out for perhaps half an hour, then rose part way up to stand on its forelegs. Finally after another half hour it rose all the way up to stand "properly" on two legs.

I called Rosi Dagit to ask if she had any possible explanation for this odd behavior. She told me that sometimes the youngsters learning to fly come down too fast and hurt themselves when they hit the ground and what we saw may have been a recovery period after a crash landing.

The other day I was returning from the box canyon at the far end of our "estate" and was reaching for the back gate when I glanced over the fence and saw one of our adult Red-tailed Hawks. He was only ten feet from me and was clutching in one foot the largest gopher I have ever seen. I was very pleased. I had been trying for over a week to catch this gopher but he systematically foiled me by dogging up my traps with dirt. I wanted to reward the hawk for doing the job for me but I couldn't figure out how to do that. I guess having all that fresh meat for his family's consumption was reward enough for him. Anyhow, he soon took off with the rodent firmly grasped in the talons of his right foot. As I watched him fly to his nest, I was hoping he might add an occasional gopher from my lawn to his regular diet.

# The Man Who Repairs Bird Wings

I know a man who repairs bird wings! Skipper is his name. He started with a dragonfly that flew into the windshield on his pickup truck. It stayed sort of plastered there so he stopped and picked it off. He discovered that one of it wings was broken. He wanted to fix it so what he tried was putting Super Glue on both sides of the wing. When the glue hardened up, the dragonfly flapped both its wings and flew away.

Next thing to get hit by his moving windshield was a butterfly. Very carefully, he again poured Super Glue over the broken areas. As soon as the glue dried, the butterfly also flapped its wings and flew away.

Then one day he found a hummingbird lying on the ground looking dead. He figured it had flown into the window it was lying under. When he picked it up, he saw it was still alive. It could sit up and looked perky, but it had a broken wing. Guess what he did? He dug out the bottle of Super Glue again and poured some on the broken part of the wing. It only took five minutes to dry. Then the hummer flapped its wings and flew away.

Note, His method has not been verified as valid by wildlife experts, so we're not able to recommend it as a life-time cure.

# Northern Hawk

A wintery landscape stretches before me. A vast snow-covered meadow bordered miles to the west by snowcapped Sierra peaks, stretches north and south all the way to the horizon.

Running through it on a winding course is the Owens River-only ten feet wide this close to its source in the mountains. It is flowing too swiftly to freeze, though ice forms wherever water laps its shores.

A small flock of Northern Pintails is dabbling in the stream. Five Common Mergansers suddenly take off in one direction, wheel in a tight turn and fly away in the other. Six Ring-billed Gulls come screaming in, swooping down to scoop morsels from the surface of the stream. A lone lark stops and starts, patrolling a bare strip of grass along the shore.

A hawk methodically works the meadow. He courses about ten feet above the ground in a quartering pattern, about a hundred yards in each direction. From time to time he interrupts his graceful flight to hover in midair for a minute or so, then flies on. Suddenly he drops, pouncing on a gopher which he quickly subdues. Holding his dying prey in one talon, he pivots his head and scans the field.

The hawk sees a Golden Eagle rise into the air a long distance down the meadow. The eagle flaps his huge wings slowly, though approaching with deceptive speed.

The hawk crouches, tensed and wary. It is already too late to fly away. The eagle circles the hawk and flies on. The gopher was probably not enough of a meal to be worth a fight.

Far up the meadow, the eagle perches on a fence post. A raven sees the eagle land and flies over to investigate. He lights on a nearby rock and studies the lion of the skies.

Seeing no sign of food about, he flies on, and discovers the hawk, which is now busy tearing its prey apart and gulping down the pieces. The raven lands near the hawk, fluffs out his throat feathers and jerks his head back and forth in what may be meant to be a menacing display. The hawk ignores him.

The raven advances slowly, begins to croak. The hawk continues to feed and to ignore the raven. The raven stops its advance just a few feet from the hawk, stands uncertainly for a moment, and flies away. I study the hawk through a tripod-mounted telescope. It has the general appearance of a Red-tailed Hawk, though its plumage is whiter than usual, and it has a black belly.

Its legs are feathered all the way to the feet, which identifies it as a Rough-legged Hawk, and reflects its adaptation to a cold climate. (I remembered from a dead one beside Route 395 that even the eyelids are covered with down to protect this bird from the cold.)

This particular Rough-legged Hawk has come down from somewhere between the Arctic Circle and the North Pole. It is one of the two raptors which make their home on the tundra.

The tundra is that magical land which circles the globe across three continents. It lies flat, bleak, and dark through most of the year, but for two or three months the sun shines almost 24 hours a day. When the snow melts, the land springs to life. Plants grow rapidly. Thousands of wolves, hundreds of thousands of caribou, millions of birds, billions of rodents, trillions of mosquitoes and multitudes of innumerable other creatures appear. Some of them come from as close as several inches under the ground. Others come from as far away as Tierra del Fuego at the bottom-most tip of South America.

Amidst all this teeming life on the tundra, the Rough-legged Hawk and the Gyrfalcon are the two raptors most at home. Their feeding habits are very different. The Rough-legged subsists on lemmings and voles while the Gyrfalcons subsist on Ptarmigan. The rodents go underground in winter, so the Rough-legged has to leave the North. Ptarmigans are abundant during the winter so the Gyrfalcons don't have to leave.

This explains why I found this arctic visitor to the Owens Valley one California winter. The vast snow covered meadows there look much like the tundra and the Rough-legged Hawk seemed quite at home.

# A Sharpy Strikes Out

The other day a simple thing happened which unexpectedly threw me into a state of momentary shock. I had been reclining on the deck in our box canyon, basking torpid in the sun, dimly aware of a Yellow-rumped Warbler flitting about our pond catching insects which were on the wing. Suddenly I was startled by a crashing sound in a bush across the pond. I saw a blur of large flashing wings, then nothing. A stillness ensued which was as alarming as the preceding crash. Neither the warbler nor the intruder was to be seen.

I felt a vague sense of terror welling up in me. I lifted binoculars to my eyes and peered into the brush, straining to see what had happened and thereby, perhaps, to restore some order to my corner of the world.

At first, I saw only a mosaic of leaves and branches and shadows against the bank before me. Then, out of the mosaic, emerged the sinister shape of a Sharp-shinned Hawk. He was perched in a bush, empty clawed. He stayed for a moment then took off down the canyon. I realized that I was disappointed that he had missed his prey.

Then I discerned the warbler sitting very still in the far end of the bush in which the hawk had perched. For five minutes or more, he kept his body hunched and rigid while he jerked his head nervously about to survey his surroundings.

As I watched the warbler, I too became a fugitive, cowering in the brush near where the predator had passed. Do we humans somehow still remember those many times when our ancestors shrank in terror while a predator prowled through the neighborhood? Was this the source of the terror which stirred in me when I first heard the crash in the brush?

# About the Author

Gerry Haigh has lived in Topanga Canyon for 46 years, but was born in New York City in 1921. He became interested in nature through the parks in that city, hoped for a career in forestry, but due to restrictions in the family budget, the only place of study available to him was City College–not so good for forestry–and so nature became a hobby.

He studied with Carl Rogers at the University of Chicago and received a PhD in psychology in 1950, going on to obtain a post-doctoral fellowshp at Menninger's, the world-famous psychiatric clinic in Topeka, Kansas.

From 1962 until retirement, Dr. Haigh was a psychotherapist with the Psychological Service Associates, Los Angeles, the first group private practice of clinical psychologists in the nation.

For many years Gerry spent three days a week at his Westwood office and four in Topanga, where he volunteered at the elementary school and with community organizations. For 30 years he led monthly birdwalks in the Santa Monica Mountains for the Audubon Society and the Sierra Club.

In 1999 the Topanga Chamber of Commerce recognized Gerry as Naturalist and Birdman of Topanga, "In Gratitude for a Lifetime of Commitment to Topanga's Wild Kingdom". His enthusiasm for the natural world has inspired hundreds of people in the Los Angeles area.

Printed in the United States
120254LV00001B/1-99/P